EXPERIMENTAL MUSIC

Experimental Music

COMPOSITION WITH AN ELECTRONIC COMPUTER

Lejaren A. Hiller, Jr.
ASSISTANT PROFESSOR OF MUSIC
SCHOOL OF MUSIC, UNIVERSITY OF ILLINOIS

Leonard M. Isaacson
MATHEMATICIAN
STANDARD OIL COMPANY OF CALIFORNIA
FORMERLY RESEARCH ASSOCIATE
UNIVERSITY OF ILLINOIS

GREENWOOD PRESS, PUBLISHERS
WESTPORT, CONNECTICUT

Library of Congress Cataloging in Publication Data

Hiller, Lejaren Arthur, 1924-
  Experimental music.

    Reprint of the ed. published by McGraw-Hill, New
York.
    1. Computer composition. I. Isaacson, Leonard
Maxwell, 1925-   joint author. II. Title.
[MT41.H58 1980]   781.6'1'02854   79-21368
ISBN 0-313-22158-8 lib. bdg.

Reprinted in 1979 by Greenwood Press, Inc.
51 Riverside Avenue, Westport, CT. 06880

Printed in the United States of America

10 9 8 7 6 5 4 3 2 1

PREFACE

In presenting this discussion of a series of unusual experiments in experimental musical composition, the authors wish to record their appreciation of numerous instances of invaluable assistance and encouragement they have had during the course of carrying out this work.

In particular, we would like to acknowledge the support and interest received from the Digital Computer Laboratory at the University of Illinois and its director, Dr. Ralph Meagher, and to make note of the encouragement we received to pursue this work from Dr. John P. Nash,[1] who, at the time this work was carried out, was Research Professor of Mathematics at the Digital Computer Laboratory in charge of programming and mathematical research. It is perhaps of interest to mention that the Digital Computer Laboratory at the University of Illinois is an independent laboratory under the direct administration of the Graduate College and among its objectives is the fostering of university research of all types for which computers can be used. In this connection, we should like to note the friendly interest in our project accorded us by Dr. Frederick T. Wall, Dean of the Graduate College. Secondly, we should like to acknowledge the assistance and interest of several members of the University of Illinois School of Music faculty. In particular, Dr. Hubert Kessler, of the composition and theory staff, has taken a direct interest in this work and the many discussions we have had with him have been invaluable in clarifying both the objectives of the work and the analysis of the experimental results obtained. Thirdly, we are indebted to Professor J. Robert Kelly, also of the composition and theory staff, not only for suggesting certain experiments in regard to the production of tone rows by means of computers, but also for helping to arrange a concert at which the first performance of the *Illiac Suite* was given. We wish to make note of the efforts of Professor Robert Swenson and the other members of the string quartet in preparing the *Illiac Suite* for the performance given at that time. We should like to acknowledge the many helpful suggestions

---

[1] Current address: Lockheed Missile Systems Division, Sunnyvale, California.

v

and criticisms we have received from many other interested friends, both within the departments mentioned and outside them. Lastly, we would like to mention the interest we received both at the inception of this work and later on from Professor Milton Babbitt, of the Department of Music at Princeton University, a friend of one of the authors, who encouraged the idea that work of this type would be of interest to contemporary composers, and from Professor Vladimir Ussachevsky, of the Department of Music at Columbia University. Professor Ussachevsky, in connection with his own studies of contemporary experimental music, made a special trip to Urbana to inquire about our work and subsequently helped arrange the initial publication of the score of the *Illiac Suite*. This has been a strong stimulus to us to complete the present task of writing, so that we may look forward to new projects which will extend the scope of the experiments to be described.

Lejaren A. Hiller, Jr.
Leonard M. Isaacson

CONTENTS

Preface v

Chapter One. Nature of the Problem 1
Introduction. Chronology. Presentation of the Material.

Two. The Aesthetic Problem 10
Meaning and Form in Music. The Logic of Musical
Composition. Information Theory. Information Theory
and Music.

Three. Experimental Music 36
Experimental Music Defined. Electronic, or Synthetic,
Music. Programmed Music. Other Experiments to Gen-
erate Computer Music.

Four. The Technical Problem 58
Non-numerical Uses of Computers. Operation of Auto-
matic High-speed Digital Computers. The "Man-versus-
Machine" Problem. The Monte Carlo Method. The
Monte Carlo Method and the Generation of Music.

Five. Experimental Details 79
Outline of Experiments. Experiment One. Experiment
Two. Experiment Three. Experiment Four.

Six. Experimental Results: The Illiac Suite 152
Introduction. Experiment One. Experiment Two. Experiment Three. Experiment Four.

Seven. Some Future Musical Applications 165
Introduction. Applications to Music Analysis. Applications to Music Composition. Summary of Results.

Appendix 181

CHAPTER ONE

Nature of the Problem

Introduction

Upon first hearing of the idea of computer music, a person might ask: "Why program a digital computer to generate music?" The answer to this question is not simple, since such an undertaking immediately raises fundamental questions concerning the nature of musical communication and its relation to formal musical structures. Moreover, it also raises the question of how far it is possible to express musical and aesthetic principles in forms suitable for computer processing. Lastly, it also brings up the problem of what role automation of the type exemplified by high-speed digital computers can be expected to fulfill in the creative arts.

We shall point out in Chapter 2 that the process of musical composition can be characterized as involving a series of choices of musical elements from an essentially limitless variety of musical raw materials. Therefore, because the act of composing can be thought of as the extraction of order out of a chaotic multitude of available possibilities, it can be studied at least semiquantitatively by applying certain mathematical operations deriving from probability theory and certain general principles of analysis incorporated in a new theory of communication called *information theory*. It becomes possible, as a consequence, to apply computers to the study of those aspects of the process of composition which can be formalized in these terms.

More specifically, when we raise this question of whether it is possible to compose music with a computer, we may note the following points: (1) Music is a sensible form. It is governed by laws of organization which permit fairly exact codification. (As we shall later note, it has even been claimed that the content of music is nothing but its organization.) From this proposition, it follows that computer-produced music which is "meaningful" is conceivable to the extent to which the laws of musical organization are codifiable. (2) It is a feature of digital computers that they can be efficiently used to "create a random universe" and to select ordered sets of information from this random universe in accordance with imposed rules, musical or otherwise. (3) Since the process of creative composition can be similarly viewed as an imposition of order upon an infinite variety of possibilities, an analogy between the two processes seems to hold, and the opportunity is afforded for a fairly close approximation of the composing process utilizing a high-speed electronic digital computer. In this context, it should be noted, however, that the composer is traditionally thought of as guided in his choices not only by certain technical rules but also by his "aural sensibility," while the computer would be dependent entirely upon a rationalization and codification of this "aural sensibility."

In order to examine this idea experimentally, we have carried out a series of experiments to determine whether automatic high-speed digital computers such as the Illiac, located at the University of Illinois, can be used to generate music subject only to general instructions derived from various specified "rules" of composition. In a computer, this is done by letting the control of the musical output be limited solely by the input instructions, and leaving factors not specifically accounted for in the input instructions entirely to chance. In general, this appeared to be an attractive new nonmathematical application of high-speed computer operation which could be of interest not only as an illustration of the versatility of these instruments but also in terms of its possible effect on the fields of musical composition and analysis.

It is desirable to consider briefly how automatic high-speed digital computers operate. These instruments function in principle much as do ordinary desk calculators, but with certain significant differences. Perhaps the most important difference is that a whole set of computing instructions, called a *code* or *computing program,* which is entirely expressed in terms of mathematical operations, and which is prepared from a library of instructions called an *order code,* is placed into a computer prior to the actual process of computation. This eliminates delays resulting from the slowness of the human operator in handling numbers being produced during the period of actual computation. A second important difference is that automatic digital computers have what is called a *conditional transfer* process. In the Illiac, this is essentially a yes-or-no choice operation which permits the programming of decisions which depend upon whether numbers bear positive or negative signs. Specifically, the instructions of a program placed into the Illiac are acted upon sequentially in the normal course of computation. However, the conditional-transfer order, whenever it is reached in this set of instructions, *may* shift the sequence of operations to another part of the program, depending upon the results of the calculations carried out to that point. A simple example of this process is the testing of a counting index for a change of sign set to occur at the termination of an iterative computation cycle.

It is operations of this type used repeatedly and sequentially, perhaps more than any other, that permit programs to be written for the computer expressing logical processes of musical composition. This happens because these two features of computers, namely, extremely high speed and the ability to react differently to positive and negative numbers, permit the practical exploitation of the so-called "Monte Carlo method" for solving certain types of complex mathematical problems. The success of the Monte Carlo method depends upon the generation of random integers in great profusion, even up to the order of millions of integers. These integers, as they are produced, are examined and sorted according to the needs of the problem to be solved, until gradually a better and better approximation to the answer to the problem is obtained.[1] To do this, the laws of probability theory are applied within the restrictions of the particular problem being studied, so that random integers not in accord with these restrictions are discarded. The method is obviously hopelessly inefficient without a device such as an automatic computer, but since these instruments have become available, the technique has been applied successfully to a number of complex problems, both within the scientific field and in other areas, as in the present instance.

We proposed that the composition of music could be treated by the Monte Carlo method. We were able to act upon this proposition by resolving the process of generating computer music into two basic opera-

[1] D. D. McCracken, "The Monte Carlo Method," *Sci. American,* 192(5):90, May, 1955.

tions. In the first operation, the computer was instructed to generate random sequences of integers which were equated to the notes of the musical scale and, in certain experiments, also to rhythmic patterns, dynamics, and playing instructions such as *arco, pizzicato,* and *col legno.* These random integers, which can be generated at a rate of up to about a thousand per second, were then processed in the second, more complex operation in which each random integer was screened through a series of arithmetic tests expressing various rules of composition and either used or rejected depending on which rules were in effect. If accepted, the random integer was used to build up a "composition" and stored in the computer until the completed "composition" was ready to be printed out. On the other hand, if it was rejected, a new random integer was generated and examined. This process was repeated until a satisfactory note was found or until it became evident that no such note existed, in which case part of the "composition" thus far composed was automatically erased to allow a fresh start.

The purely technical problems involved in programming the computer to process musical information were soon seen to be the part of the total problem which would inevitably preoccupy us during the earlier parts of the investigation. Technical decisions of many types would necessarily outweigh in importance subtler aesthetic considerations. Therefore, the logical sequence of experiments seemed to be the following: (1) To select some simple but well-known style of writing and use this as a basis to build up an elementary technique of polyphonic writing. A simplified version of first-species strict counterpoint was utilized for this purpose. (2) Then, once many of the technical problems of coding had been worked out in this way, to demonstrate that standard musical techniques could be handled by computer programming, so that conventional musical output, recognizable to musicians, is produced. The solution of the basic problems of first-species strict counterpoint was, therefore, carried out to produce *cantus firmus* settings which were academically correct in all their most important details. (3) To demonstrate that a computer can produce novel musical structures in a more contemporary style and to code musical elements such as rhythm and dynamics. This was done to show that computers might be used by contemporary composers to extend present compositional techniques. (4) To show, lastly, that computers might be used in highly unusual ways to produce radically different species of music based upon fundamentally new techniques of musical analysis. In this last experiment, a complete departure from traditional compositional practice is illustrated.

Computer output produced as a result of carrying out these four experiments was utilized to produce a four-movement piece of music we have entitled the *Illiac Suite for String Quartet*. This is a transcription organized into four movements which parallel the sequence of experiments just described. The musical materials in these four movements were taken from a much larger body of material by unbiased sampling procedures, so that a representative rather than a selectively chosen musically superior group of results would be included in the *Illiac Suite*. Thus, it is important to realize when examining this score that our primary aim was not the presentation of an aesthetic unity—a work of art. This music was meant to be a research record—a laboratory notebook. The complete score of the *Illiac Suite* has been recently published[2] and is reproduced by permission of the original publishers in the Appendix.

This brief introductory description we have given of certain features of the production of computer music can now be used to provoke certain questions relevant to the question of generating computer music. Specifically, the first question we can raise is this: Are there ways to investigate music in a quantitative way to reveal more precisely the relationship of musical textures to conceptual frameworks which seem to be significant in musical composition? Secondly, in a more restricted sense, can we investigate through certain types of analysis of musical forms the general logical foundation a composer uses to build up a musical composition? Thirdly, can we use automatic high-speed digital computers to aid a study involving these questions? And lastly, might this also lead to new and different ways of composing music which would interest the contemporary composer?

Chronology

Actual work on this problem was started in September, 1955, at which time the present authors decided to collaborate to write the initial computer programs for producing music. The initial set of instructions was designed to cause the Illiac to generate simple *cantus firmi;* that is, simple diatonic melodies to be utilized subsequently to produce simple polyphony. Both authors had worked previously on Monte Carlo-type problems in connec-

[2] L. A. Hiller, Jr. and L. M. Isaacson, *Illiac Suite for String Quartet*, New Music Edition, 30:3, 1957.

tion with another research project and thus had had previous experience with coding problems of this type for a computer. In fact, a sizable portion of the basic programming techniques of the earlier music codes for the Illiac was adapted from this earlier research. The work as previously outlined progressed very smoothly, so that, by the following spring, we had accumulated enough material to begin the assembly of a musical record of the research results in the form of the *Illiac Suite*. By July, 1956, the first three movements of the suite had been completed with the exception of what is now the Coda of the third movement. A performance of this much of the suite was given publicly on August 9, 1956, at a concert at the University of Illinois in Urbana, Illinois. This performance, which was privately recorded at the same time, was by a string quartet composed of Robert Swenson, cellist with the Walden String Quartet resident at the University of Illinois, and three instrumentalists, Sanford Reuning, violin, Peggy Andrix, violin, and George Andrix, viola, who were at that time graduate students in the University of Illinois School of Music. This concert attracted considerable attention because of its novelty, and representative reports of this event both prior to it and afterwards in the popular press can be cited to indicate the extent and nature of the reaction which occurred.[3, 4]

This was followed shortly thereafter by a public presentation of some of our experimental work during a symposium on non-numerical uses for digital computers at the 11th National Meeting of the Association for Computing Machinery on August 28, 1956,[5, 6] and since then we have given several other oral presentations of aspects of this research.[7] In the

[3] Locally, P. Cahill, "Illiac—Mechanical Brain—Takes Up Composing Music," *Champaign-Urbana News Gazette,* July 8, 1956; P. Cahill, "Illiac Proves Music Skill," *ibid.,* Aug. 10, 1956; R. Starr, "Illiac Tackles the Arts," *Champaign-Urbana Courier,* Aug. 10, 1956.

[4] More generally, U. P. News release, Aug. 10, 1956, concerning concert reprinted nationally in many newspapers; I. Wilheim, " 'Brain' Makes like Bach for Scientists," *Washington Post,* Sept. 2, 1956; Anon., "By the Numbers," *Musical America,* 76:13, September, 1956; A. Carpenter, "Amazing New Uses for Robot Brains," *Sci. Digest,* 41(2):1, February, 1957.

[5] L. A. Hiller, Jr. and L. M. Isaacson, "Musical Composition with a Digital Computer," Program and Abstracts for the 11th National Meeting of the Association for Computing Machinery, University of California at Los Angeles, Aug. 27–29, 1956, p. 8 and p. 22.

[6] E. Cony, "Canny Computers: Machines Write Music, Play Checkers, Tackle New Tasks in Industry," *Wall St. Journal,* Sept. 19, 1956. This is a general report of the convention.

[7] L. A. Hiller, Jr., "The Generation of Music by High-speed Digital Computers," Meeting of Chicago Section, Institute of Radio Engineers, Chicago, Dec. 7, 1956; ab-

meanwhile, during the fall months of 1956, the Coda of the third movement of the *Illiac Suite* was finished, and the experiments which now make
up the fourth movement were carried out to complete the work included
in the *Illiac Suite* by the end of November, 1956. Not long thereafter,
through the interest of Vladimir Ussachevsky, Chairman of the Editorial
Board of *New Music Editions,* a quarterly for publishing new musical compositions, the publication, already referred to,[1] of the complete score of the
Illiac Suite was arranged. This left one major task to carry out besides
recording the work in its entirety, which was the preparation of a published
account of the research work embodied in the *Illiac Suite.*

Presentation of the Material

When the time arrived to write a record of the experiments carried out
with the Illiac, it became evident that enough material had accumulated so
that a highly condensed presentation no longer seemed adequate; the variety
of problems considered during the course of the research had become quite
extensive. Moreover, it seemed important to present enough details so that
the precise extent of what was done would be clearly understood. This
research cuts across fields of interest normally considered discretely separate. Rather than break up the material and publish part of it in a form
specifically directed to a reader with a musical background and another
part directed to the reader with a background in applied mathematics, we
preferred to prepare one single discussion of the work which would be
reasonably complete and self-contained. Thus, we have included what we
feel is relevant material on experimental music, musical aesthetics, and
related topics. These discussions are required to define and differentiate
the problem in musical terms with sufficient accuracy. It seems sufficient
to point out that unless aesthetic considerations are taken into account,
projects of this type tend to turn out rather poorly. Because of this reason,
significant technical advances in the art fields too often have been over-

---

stract in *Scanfax,* 10:7, 1956; L. A. Hiller, Jr., "Some Structural Principles of Computer Music," Annual meeting of the Midwestern Chapter of the American Musicological Society at Michigan State University, East Lansing, Mich., May 19, 1957;
abstract to be published in *J. Am. Musicological Soc.;* L. A. Hiller, Jr. and L. M.
Isaacson, "Musical Composition with a High-speed Digital Computer," 9th Annual
Convention of the Audio Engineering Society, New York, October 10, 1957; also
J. Audio Eng. Soc. in press; L. A. Hiller, Jr., "Musique Électronique," *Encyclopédie
des sciences modernes,* VIII, Éditions René Kister, Geneva, Switzerland, 1958, pp.
110–112.

looked for too long a time by creative artists, since the innovators have taken insufficient pains to evaluate what is artistically significant in their work to present their materials in the best way. Certain contemporary experiments in synthetic music discussed in Chapter 3 are cases in point. Secondly, it is necessary that our discussion of the technical details of coding musical problems for the computer be sufficiently detailed to be understood by the musician who could not be expected to have acquired a specialized knowledge of computers and how they are used. It is one of our primary aims to demonstrate to musicians that the basic techniques for applying these instruments to musical problems are simple in their essence and that an extensive scientific background is not required to use them. Lastly, we are also aware of the problem of misinformation concerning computers and automation. To illustrate, we might consider a passage from a recent book on automation:[8]

[In] an American public opinion poll in Detroit, people were asked to fill up forms writing down their fears in order of magnitude. The subject which headed the poll was fear of Russia, but to the surprise of the organizers the second greatest fear was "fear of automation." This surprising and indeed disturbing result shows how great a fear of the unknown can become. A fire, started by the press in a sensational manner, fanned by science fiction writers, poked by agitators, and with fuel added by a slight recession in the car industry, had clearly got out of hand. But there is this interesting aspect: few of the people either writing or speaking on the subject were giving the word "automation" the same meaning. Even so, the word became a bogy. It had become the cliché of the year. The American man-in-the-street obviously could not understand the welter of information and distortions that were directed at him and naturally concluded that the whole thing was beyond his understanding but that its effects were evil. He did not suspect that the writers and speakers were of doubtful quality.

Obviously, this whole experience can easily be transcribed to other areas in which automation is having an impact and indeed could arise also in regard to the present work. With this point in mind, we will also discuss in general terms how computers work and what may be expected in the near future in their specific application to musical problems. Naturally, if applications in the musical field are to be of significance, it is to be expected that problems will arise which will challenge the ingenuity of contemporary composers and musicians, but this is as it should be, since it is

[8] L. L. Goodman, *Man and Automation,* Penguin Books, Inc., Baltimore, 1957, p. 169.

not in the nature of a vital art form to remain aesthetically static and insensitive to technological change. Our plan in writing this book, therefore, is not only just to present the bare outline of the particular experiments carried out by means of the Illiac, but also to fill in enough details so that a reasonably complete picture of the potentialities of this research might be realized.

A reasonable organization of the material seemed to be the following: (1) To introduce aesthetic limits to the problem, that is, to define what can be accomplished musically with a computer at the present time, and to define what is—at the moment at least—outside the scope of available experimental tools. This is the purpose of Chapter 2. To clarify this problem, we have included a brief discussion of information theory, the theoretical basis of our method, which should serve as a bridge to the material that follows. (2) To define the area of research musically, that is, to distinguish these experiments from and to correlate them with other types of musical experiments both of the past and now in progress. This is the purpose of Chapter 3. (3) To consider, in Chapter 4, technical problems. In this discussion, we are basically concerned with two subjects; the first being a description of how modern computers operate, and the second being a general discussion of the mathematical methods used to set up the problem of generating computer music. (4) The next two chapters of the book contain detailed descriptions of the experimental techniques and the experimental results. In Chapter 5, the programming techniques for the various musical problems studied are reviewed in considerable detail, while in Chapter 6, a description and an evaluation of the contents of the *Illiac Suite* are given. (5) Finally, in Chapter 7, we suggest a number of possible extensions of this work in the fields of music analysis and music composition.

CHAPTER TWO

The Aesthetic Problem

Meaning and Form in Music

Two questions which often arise when music is discussed are, on the one hand, the substance of musical communication, its symbolic and semantic significance, if any, and on the other hand, the particular processes, both mental and technical, which are involved in creating and responding to musical compositions. These two basic problems have been, of course, subjected to exhaustive discussion throughout recorded history, to no slight extent because of the difficulties involved in demonstrating how music acquires "significance." Because music has fewer tangible models in nature from which artists can work, it has often been suggested that meaning and coherence in music are achieved by more purely formal procedures than are usually applied in either the graphic or literary arts. It is not our purpose to examine this problem in detail, but rather only to define musical terms so that reasonable limits for the experiments to generate computer music may be established in musical terms.

As is well known, the nature of musical communication has been discussed by writers at least as far back as Plato and Aristotle, or the even earlier Pythagoreans. The earliest writers saw in music an *imitation* of a fundamental *divine harmony* of universal significance. Music was felt to bring *harmony* to the body and soul through such elements as melody and rhythm. Aristotle examined music more directly and suggested that it is an external manifestation of inward emotional and moral states. For example, in Problem 29,[1] he suggested that music imitates "movements of the soul" and "moral character." He asks: "Why do rhythms and tunes, which after all are only voice, resemble moral characters (i.e., the feelings) . . . ? Is it because they are movements, as actions also are?"

Ever since these earliest writers, music has been a subject of considerable fascination to philosophers and mathematicians, even often being classified as a form of mathematics and thus considered to reveal natural law in terms of mathematical logic. For example, Cassiodorus (ca. 485–ca. 575) defined the mathematical *quadrivium* as follows:[2]

Mathematical science is that science which considers abstract quantity. By abstract quantity we mean that quantity which we treat in a purely speculative way, separating it intellectually from its material and from its other accidents, such as evenness, oddness, and the like. It has these divisions: arithmetic, music, geometry, astronomy. Arithmetic is the discipline of absolute numerable quantity. Music is the discipline which treats of numbers in their relation to those things which are found in sound. . . .

If this attitude strikes many of us as a bit peculiar today, perhaps it is only a result of being conditioned to think of music so completely in terms of its supposed emotional appeal. The still-popular concept of music as a direct emotional expression and an explicit and subjective communication from the composer is, in fact, largely a consequence of the rather extreme views developed during the period of the nineteenth-century Romantic tradition. Nineteenth-century composers, whose works still make up a large part of the standard repertory, often themselves felt this way about their music. The more articulate of these composers, such as Berlioz,[3] Wagner,[4] and Busoni,[5] to cite specific examples, were quite explicit in their attitudes

[1] W. D. Ross (ed.), *The Works of Aristotle,* vol. 7, *Problemata* (trans. by E. S. Forster), Oxford University Press, New York, 1927, book XIX.

[2] Cassiodorus, *Institutiones,* II, iii, paragraph 21, as quoted in O. Strunk, *Source Readings in Music History,* W. W. Norton & Company, Inc., New York, 1950, p. 88, footnote 6.

[3] H. Berlioz, *A travers Chants, études musicales, adorations, boutades, et critiques,* Michel Levy, Paris, 1862, and other writings.

[4] R. Wagner, *Das Kunstwerk der Zukunft,* 1850, relevant passages in Strunk, *op. cit.,* pp. 874–903, in particular, p. 881.

[5] F. Busoni, *Sketch of a New Aesthetic of Music,* 1907 (trans. by T. Baker), G. Schirmer, New York, 1911; also F. Busoni, *The Essence of Music and Other*

and spoke of music as the direct communication "from heart to heart"; of tone as "the direct expression of feeling" (Wagner); of the need for "emotional sensitivity" (Berlioz); of the role of music as dealing with the interpretation of human feelings, the portrayal of "soul states"; and of the necessity of music not being fettered by pedantic forms (Busoni). On the other hand, it is interesting to note, by contrast, that Stravinsky, for example, has recently restated the more traditional definition of music in emphatic terms when he characterized "the phenomenon of music as a form of speculation in terms of sound and time."[6] It should be clearly understood, however, that sound and time are for Stravinsky sensuous elements, not physico-mathematical abstractions.

This speculation, moreover, is a unique language, like each significant art form, which has validity precisely because its most significant levels of meaning are not translatable into words. We might note that Helmholtz[7] considers this problem when he reflects Aristotle's concepts of the relation of music toward internal mental and emotional states by stating that:

Every motion is an expression of the power which produces it, and we instinctively measure the motive force by the amount of motion which it produces. . . . In this way melodic progression can become the expression of the most diverse conditions of human disposition, not precisely of human *feelings*, but at least of that *state of sensitiveness* which is produced by feelings . . . [of] that general character temporarily shown by the motion of our conceptions. . . . Words can represent the cause of the frame of mind, the object to which it refers, and the feeling which lies at its root, while music expresses the kind of mental transition which is due to the feeling. . . . Music does not represent feelings and situations, but only frames of mind which the hearer is unable to describe except by adducing such outward circumstances as he has himself noticed when experiencing the corresponding mental states. . . . In this sense, Vischer's[8] rather paradoxical statement that the mechanics of mental emotion are perhaps best studied in their expression in music may not be altogether incorrect.

Perhaps the most significant idea contained in Helmholtz's remarks is

Papers (trans. by R. Ley), Rockliff, London, 1957, for a general collection of Busoni's music writings.

  [6] I. Stravinsky, *Poetics of Music*, Harvard University Press, Cambridge, Mass.. 1947, p. 16.

  [7] H. L. M. Helmholtz, *On the Sensations of Tone*, 2d English edition of 1885 by A. J. Ellis, based on the 4th German edition of 1877, Dover Publications, New York, 1954, p. 250 *et seq.*

  [8] Helmholtz is referring to a passage from F. T. von Vischer, *Aesthetik, Wissenschaft des Schönen*, C. Mäcken, Stuttgart, 1858.

the definition of music as an external tonal representation of the "orderly motion of our conceptions." Secondly, Helmholtz's comments also illustrate his awareness of the difficulty of trying to attach literal meanings to musical materials. These two problems have been examined also by more recent writers. For example, Susanne Langer,[9] who believes that music has "significant form," examines various well-known aesthetic theories such as music being primarily pure formal design, as argued by Hanslick,[10] music being primarily self-expression, music being primarily a pleasurable experience, and so on, and rejects each as insufficient *in itself* to account for the artistic merit of musical experiences. This, we might note in passing, is rather an injustice to Hanslick and Helmholtz, both of whom anticipate many of Langer's ideas. In any event, Langer suggests that:

If music has any merit, it is semantic, not symptomatic. . . . If it has any emotional content, it "has" it in the same sense that language "has" its conceptual content—*symbolically*. It is not usually derived *from* affects nor intended *for* them . . . it is *about* them. Music is . . . their *logical expression*. . . . For what music can actually reflect is only the morphology of feeling . . . music conveys *general forms* of feelings, related to specific ones as algebraic expressions are related to arithmetic [expressions]. . . . What most aestheticians failed to see [in music] is its intellectual value, its close relation to concepts, not by reason of its difficult academic laws but in virtue of its *revelations*.

Langer concludes that: ". . . Articulation is its life, but not assertion . . . a significant form without conventional significance. . . ."

These definitions of meaning and form in music have been examined in greater detail by Langer in a more recent publication[11] without, however, significant additions. Unfortunately, Langer is not particularly concerned with musical materials as such. Therefore, a somewhat similar analysis, more relevant to the musician's concern with his materials, is contained in Meyer's recently published book on the aesthetic content in music.[12] Meyer, in contrast to Langer, attempts to relate musical meaning and musical experience to specific musical forms. He does not, as do many writers, retain the separation between "absolute" and "referential" musical

[9] S. Langer, *Philosophy in a New Key*, New American Library, New York, 1948, pp. 165–199.

[10] E. Hanslick, *The Beautiful in Music*, first publ. 1854, English edition of 1891 by J. Cohen, based on 7th German edition of 1885, The Liberal Arts Press, New York, 1957.

[11] S. Langer, *Feeling and Form*, Philosophical Library, Inc., New York, 1953.

[12] L. B. Meyer, *Emotion and Meaning in Music*, University of Chicago Press, Chicago, 1956.

meanings—he points out that musical meaning depends upon learned responses to musical stimuli—nor does he retain the classic distinction between the "emotional" and "intellectual" content of music, which has been utilized as a working principle by even so recent a writer as Hindemith.[13] Meyer instead proposes an "affect theory of music," based upon the concept that emotion is evolved when a tendency to respond is inhibited. Thus, in music, "the relationship between the tendency and its necessary resolution is made explicit and apparent."[14] Meyer remarks that music arouses expectations, some conscious and others unconscious, which may or may not be directly and immediately satisfied,[15] and then relates meaning and emotion into one unified response situation by stating that "what a musical stimulus or a series of stimuli indicate and point to are not extramusical concepts and objects but other musical events which are about to happen. . . . Embodied musical meaning is, in short, a product of expectation."[16] Meyer, starting from this premise, then examines in considerable detail significant elements of musical structure, such as "structural gaps," the "principle of saturation," and the "principle of return," as well as more familiar concepts such as tonality, rhythm, meter, and so on, in order to apply this affect theory of musical response.

In so far as referential meaning is concerned, and such concepts as Langer's "significant form" seem to fall in this category, Meyer has this to say:[17]

(1) In most cultures, there is a powerful tendency to associate musical experience with extramusical experience. . . . (2) No particular connotation is an inevitable product of a given musical organization, since the association of a specific musical organization with a particular referential experience depends upon the beliefs and attitudes of the culture toward the experience.

Although Meyer's analysis of the psychological response to musical forms and the dependence of musical form, conversely, upon psychological phenomena is perhaps one of the more interesting studies of the problem of musical content yet to come along, it is perhaps desirable, despite its value, for us for purely practical reasons to adopt as a working premise a somewhat more conservative and limited point of view. Therefore, if we

[13] P. Hindemith, *The Composer's World*, Harvard University Press, Cambridge, Mass., 1952, in particular chaps. 2 and 3.

[14] Meyer, *op. cit.*, pp. 22–23.

[15] *Ibid.*, p. 25.

[16] *Ibid.*, p. 35.

[17] *Ibid.*, p. 262.

restrict ourselves to the general definition of music as the logical expression
of inward mental and emotional states, we may also distinguish sufficiently
for our purposes between *what* music communicates and *how* music is put
together to say effectively what it has to say. Then, since the techniques
of musical composition have been treated and codified by many theoreticians in discursive and practical terms, the logical treatment of musical
materials as such can be discussed in terms of language with considerable
precision. As also noted in a recent article by Hans Tischler,[18] this aspect
of musical aesthetics was not really considered by Langer at all. He points
out that nowhere in Langer's discussion are criteria really set up for dis-
tinguishing "good music" from "bad music." Tischler states that an aesthetic appreciation of music must be based also upon a familiarity with
the medium and its technical possibilities. He notes that an entire system
of internal relations lies embedded in the medium and criticizes Langer's
preoccupation with what music appears to symbolize, stating that "to over-
look or understate this fact means pulling the basis from underneath any
aesthetic theory." He observes that Hanslick was emphatic in stressing this
point, and we might also observe that Stravinsky too complains about this
type of criticism when he says: "What is the use, in a word, of tormenting
him [the composer] with the *why* instead of seeking for itself the *how,* and
thus establishing the reasons for his failure or success?" [19]

Tischler defines two species of relationships which characterize what he
calls "multirelational aesthetics," namely:

1. *Internal Relations.* These change with the medium and in music consist of rhythm, melody, harmony, counterpoint, tone color, expression (dynamics, tempo, etc.), and form or contour.

2. *External Relations.* These are true of all the arts and consist of
gesture, program, ethics, technical mastery, psychological drives of the
artist, function (e.g., for dance, worship, etc.), relevant historical and
sociological data, and performance.

Tischler proposes that the greater the number of relationships a work of
art reveals, the greater aesthetic significance we must attach to the particular
work of art. Whether or not this is true, for our purposes, Tischler's separation of internal relationships from external relationships is extremely
useful because it separates what we can find explicitly in a musical score
from what we must read into a score in order to become aware of its more
general referential significance. Moreover, in the long run, it may be also

[18] H. Tischler, "The Aesthetic Experience," *The Music Review,* 17:189, 1956.
[19] Stravinsky, *op. cit.,* p. 87.

true that the study of musical forms will be a convenient medium for investigating the dependence of semantic meanings upon the articulation of formal structures. It is important to note, however, that the semantic properties of music do not necessarily carry over to other forms of communication, because many of the properties of music seem to depend, in considerable degree, specifically upon the medium itself.

The Logic of Musical Composition

There are five basic principles involved in musical composition which we shall consider in the present context to be of primary significance. The first principle is that the formation of a piece of music is an ordering process in which specified musical elements are selected and arranged from an infinite variety of possibilities, i.e., from *chaos*. The second principle recognizes the contribution to a musical structure not only of *order*, but also the relative lack thereof, and even, in certain extreme cases, of the absence of order, namely, *chaos;* that is to say, the degree of imposed order is itself a significant variable. The third principle is that the two most important dimensions of music upon which a greater or lesser degree of order can be imposed are pitch and time.[20] There are, of course, other necessary elements of music as ordinarily considered by the composer such as dynamic level and timbre, which also require ordering, but these will, for purposes of simplification, be considered less significant. Next, because music exists in time, the fourth principle is that memory, as well as instantaneous perception, is required in the understanding of musical structures. Lastly, as a fifth principle, it is proposed that *tonality,* a significant ordering concept, be considered the result of establishing pitch order in terms of memory recall.

The first principle, namely, that the process of musical composition involves the choice of musical elements from an essentially limitless variety of musical raw materials, has long received widespread recognition. In fact, the very name composition suggests an act of arranging, of an imposition of order, while the use of the word composer to characterize the writer of music suggests a person who assembles and builds forms. Indeed, the basic idea of composition as the extraction of *order* from *chaos* was

[20] A more generalized picture of musical structure is that of wave-form amplitude versus time. This concept lies at the root of experiments to synthesize musical structures directly on film, for example. See p. 44.

formulated as long ago as the fourth century B.C. by Aristoxenus,[21] who remarked that: "The voice follows a natural law in its motion and does not place the intervals at random." Aristoxenus also recognized the necessity of the ordering process in both music and language when he stated that: "The order that distinguishes the melodious from the unmelodious resembles that which we find in the collocation of letters in language. For it is not every collocation but only certain collocations of any given letters that will produce a syllable."

This concept of opposing order and design to chaos has been a critical issue in musical aesthetics ever since. If we limit ourselves to current writers, we may note that Igor Stravinsky, in particular, has been most explicit in his defense of this principle. It is, in fact, the central theme of his *Poetics of Music,* previously referred to.[6] Several representative passages from this book can be quoted to illustrate this point. For example, he remarks that: ". . . we feel [the necessity] to bring order out of chaos, to extricate the straight line of our operation from the tangle of possibilities";[22] that: ". . . we have recourse to what we call *order* . . . order and discipline." [23] Stravinsky also defines art as the ". . . contrary of chaos. It never gives itself up to chaos without immediately finding its living works, its very existence threatened." [24] Stravinsky stresses the point that: "Tonal elements become music only by virtue of their being organized . . . so that to the gifts of nature are added the benefits of artifice." [25] Finally, he says that: ". . . to proceed by elimination—to know how to *discard* . . . that is the great technique of selection." [26]

Given, therefore, that order is imposed during musical composition, the second question immediately arises of *how much* order is imposed. Once we recognize that all composition involves the selection of certain materials out of a random environment toward order of one sort or another, we can then ask the question of how much selection is involved in any particular process, since it is obvious that all music falls somewhere between the two extremes of order and chaos and that changes in musical style involve fluctuations first toward one pole and then toward the other. Thus, "shape

[21] Aristoxenus, *The Harmonics* (ed. and trans. by H. S. Macran), Oxford University Press, New York, 1902.
[22] Stravinsky, *op. cit.,* p. 5.
[23] *Ibid.,* p. 6.
[24] *Ibid.,* p. 11.
[25] *Ibid.,* pp. 23–24.
[26] *Ibid.,* p. 69.

may, from this point of view, be regarded as a kind of stylistic 'mean' lying between the extremes of overdifferentiation and primordial homogeneity." [27] It follows from this argument, as Meyer notes,[28] that:

Weak, ambiguous shapes may perform a valuable and vital function . . . for the lack of distinct and tangible shapes and of well-articulated modes of progression is capable of arousing powerful desires for, and expectations of, clarification and improvement. This aspect of musical structure and expression is one which has unfortunately received but scant attention from music theorists, aestheticians and critics who have continually construed "inevitability" to mean unequivocal progression. . . . Yet the fact of the matter is that some of the greatest music is great precisely because the composer has not feared to let his music tremble on the brink of chaos, thus inspiring the listener's awe, apprehension and anxiety, and, at the same time, exciting his emotions and his intellect.

The above passages, quoted from the recent study of musical meaning by Leonard Meyer, already referred to earlier, are a distinct contrast to discussions of the pair of opposites, order and chaos, which tend to confuse these terms with stylistic problems, if not also with problems of value. Thus, order has frequently been associated with "classicism" and its equivalents, and disorder with "romanticism" or "expressiveness." It is not necessary for our purposes to assess the *value* of order or of chaos as such, as Stravinsky does when he associates order with "the good," or as other composers such as John Cage, to cite a recent example, have attempted to do when they have set up an opposing musical aesthetic in which randomness or disorder is sought after as a desirable goal. The difficulty, obviously, is that few writers have attempted to define just what *order* is quantitatively in musical terms and have usually simply related this term in one way or another to compositional procedures which satisfy their stylistic prejudices. Moreover, few of them have ever considered it explicitly as a quantitative variable, subject to control for expressive purposes.

In considering specific examples of how ordering processes are imposed upon musical materials, we shall postulate that the most important involves choices of pitch. There are necessarily many such choices in musical composition. In the first place, one of the most fundamental is the decision to tune a scale to certain fixed pitches. The mere fact that most Western music is written for a chromatic scale tuned to even temperament is in itself a highly restrictive limitation upon random choice. The choice of a

[27] Meyer, *op. cit.,* p. 161.
[28] *Ibid.,* p. 160.

certain harmonic style imposes additional restrictions. Arguments in discussions of musical style, though seldom expressed explicitly as such, are really concerned in many ways with the question of how restrictive the selection process should be. Thus, stylistic limits in terms of pitch, for example, are easy to distinguish. Complete disorder is characterized by the random choice of any number of all possible pitches. On the other hand, complete order is characterized by the arbitrary and sole choice of some one fixed pitch.

A second basic choice process is connected with the fact that music, like language, depends upon a series of *successive* selections; in other words, that it exists in time. In fact, it is generally acknowledged that the two most fundamental dimensions of music specifically are pitch and time. The essential process of musical composition, therefore, consists of the sequential selection of a series of pitches. This process is also recognized by musicians, and again for comment, we may note that Stravinsky states that: "Music is based on temporal succession and requires alertness of memory. Consequently, music is a *chronologic* art, as painting is a *spatial* art." [29] Just as the restrictions imposed upon pitch selection lead to scales and ultimately to harmony, we find that restrictions of choice can be imposed upon the time dimension as well. This leads directly to the development of meter and rhythm and ultimately to the organization of large-scale musical structures. Moreover, the interaction of pitch selection and time-interval selection is the basis of virtually all our known procedures for musical composition involving the internal relationships tabulated by Tischler.

To illustrate these points, we might consider the composition of a single melodic line, restricting our argument, as we shall throughout for the sake of simplicity, to a fixed tuning scheme, specifically, the ordinary chromatic scale. We note initially that a melodic line is a sequence of *intervals* between successive notes chosen sequentially in a time scale dictated by the choice, random or otherwise, of meter and rhythm, and that it is the sequence of *intervals* rather than of tones, or *specific pitches,* which gives a melody its characteristic profile. If a mechanism is provided whereby the successive choice of intervals can be made completely random, a random melody is produced. On the other hand, if no choice whatever is provided, the melody is a monotone. The imposition of a characteristic style between these extremes involves the choice of specific rules of melodic writing which will govern the nature of successive interval selection.

Polyphony involves the simultaneous interaction of two or more melodic

[29] Stravinsky, *op. cit.,* p. 29.

lines and as such is a characteristic feature of music as distinguished from language. However, the principles of operation remain fundamentally similar, and to handle the more complex problems involved in this interaction, we require the imposition of rules of harmony and counterpoint. In the last passage we quoted from Stravinsky's *Poetics of Music,* there is mentioned another significant issue that requires comment, namely, that "music . . . requires alertness of memory." This remark points up the fact that recognition of a musical message and, hence, the over-all organization of a musical structure depends on its existence in *time* and on comprehending it in its totality in spite of its existence in time. Musical understanding has been recognized since ancient times to involve the perception of what is going on in the immediate present, but always within the framework of what has already happened and persists in the memory. For example, Aristoxenus stated that:[30] "musical cognition implies the simultaneous recognition of a permanent and a changeable element . . . for the apprehension of music depends upon these two faculties, sense perception and memory; for we must perceive the sound that is present, and remember that which is past. In no other way can we follow the phenomenon of music. . . ." St. Augustine[31] also described musical communication in these same terms when he said that listening to music depends not only on *numeri sonantes,* that is, actual music which is heard, but also upon its comparison with *numeri recordabiles,* that is, music which is remembered. This process is required in order to form a musical judgment.

The consequence of this last characteristic of musical organization is of the greatest significance, since it is at the root of our concepts and techniques of thematic repetition and development, rhythmic repetition, the need for systematic structures such as sonata form, fugue, and variation form, and, perhaps most important of all, of our ideas of tonality. Since certain experiments carried out with the Illiac involve investigation into aspects of the nature of tonality, this brings up the last point we shall consider at this stage, namely, a working definition for tonality. We shall define tonality as tonal organization based on a pitch reference point for a piece of music. A composition which uses a fixed-pitch reference point can be said to be *tonal;* if it has several such fixed reference points, it may be called *polytonal.* It is also presumably possible for the reference point to shift during the course of a composition. Lastly, if no such reference

[30] Aristoxenus, *op. cit.,* pp. 27–30.
[31] St. Augustine, *De Musica,* books I–VI (trans. by R. C. Taliaferro), The St. John's Bookstore, Annapolis, Md., 1939.

point is ascertainable, the piece can be considered *atonal*. Again, we shall not attempt to evaluate tonality as something "good" or "bad," but we shall rather treat it as a parameter to be measured and to be controlled. Moreover, if tonality in one form or another is being used to infuse coherence into a piece of music, *tones,* that is, *specific pitches, acquire significance because they are related, through specific intervals over a span of time, to a specific tonal center.* It is these long-range intervallic relationships that require memory for their recognition and which are used to build up both small- and large-scale musical structures depending upon tonal coherence as an organizational principle. It is important to separate this principle from successive interval relationships which depend much more directly only upon immediate sense perception. It is this, probably, that Aristoxenus had in mind when he remarked:[32] "Again, since intervals are not in themselves sufficient to distinguish notes—the third part of our science will deal with notes [and] will consider the question of whether they are certain points of pitch, as commonly supposed, or whether they are musical functions." In spite of this early awareness of the problem, however, it is interesting to note that, historically, the concept of tonality was one of the last to be formalized in terms of conscious operating principles and can be said to be utilized consciously in its full scope perhaps only since the time of Rameau and Bach. The rules of strict counterpoint, for example, which are based largely on the compositional techniques of the Renaissance and, specifically, the sixteenth century, are almost entirely concerned with problems of successive intervals relationships and only marginally with the question of tonality. "Sixteenth-century theorists characteristically faced the problem of chord progression as if they wore blinders that prevented them from seeing more than two chords at a time. The extent of their scope was the passage of one consonance to the next, the suspension and 'saving' of dissonances, and cadence patterns made up usually of two intervals or chords."[33] Even today, in the teaching of the theory of music, and specifically in the teaching of common practice harmony, the general problem of tonal organization is largely ignored. Basic harmony in many traditional harmony textbooks is still taught largely in terms of four-part chorale settings in the style of Bach, but with an emphasis solely on the rules of successive chord progression. It is in recognition of the lack of awareness of the necessity of utilizing logical processes

[32] Aristoxenus, *op. cit.,* p. 29.
[33] C. V. Palisca, "Vincenzo Galilei's Counterpoint Treatise: A Code for the Seconda Pratica," *J. Am. Musicological Soc.,* 4:81, 1956.

which depend upon and stimulate long-range recall that music analysts such as Heinrich Schenker (1868–1935), for example, have attempted to formulate more general principles of tonality and of melodic construction in music written since 1700 (see Chapter 5, pages 133 to 134).

To summarize, (1) the process of musical composition requires the selection of musical materials out of a random environment. This is accomplished by a process of elimination. The extent of order imposed depends upon the nature of the restrictions imposed during the process of selection. (2) Music is organized in terms of pitch—specifically, intervals between notes—and in terms of time. Many possible interactions between these two variables are expressed in terms of traditional rules of composition. (3) Musical coherence in a musical structure depends on the exploitation of memory as well as immediate sense perception. A recognition of this principle is essential in the understanding of how proper articulation is achieved in setting up musical structures.

Information Theory

In recent years, a new scientific theory, which has received the name *information theory,* or *communication theory,* has been worked out in considerable detail, particularly in certain practical applications in the fields of telegraphy, telephony, and, in general, in problems of communication engineering. We shall now consider certain important concepts of information theory relevant to the general musical problems just reviewed and in anticipation of some of the techniques applied to generate computer music. The present discussion of information theory is abstracted primarily from two recent and authoritative books on the subject by Shannon and Weaver[34] and by Brillouin.[35]

Information theory depends upon a precise and limited definition of the word *information* which answers the question of how to define the *quantity* of information contained in a message to be transmitted. As a first step toward an answer, it is observed that for the communications engineer the technical problem is always the same, namely, to transmit "information" accurately and correctly, quite without regard to the "meaning" or "value" of the "information." It is of no concern to the engineer whether the mes-

[34] C. E. Shannon and W. Weaver, *The Mathematical Theory of Communication,* University of Illinois Press, Urbana, Ill., 1949.

[35] L. Brillouin, *Science and Information Theory,* Academic Press, Inc., New York, 1956.

sage he transmits is nonsense or of the greatest significance. Therefore, in its current state, modern communication theory is restricted strictly to the study of the technical problems involved in transmitting a message from sender to receiver. Having accepted this limitation, we may then establish, as our second premise, that *every constraint imposed on freedom of choice immediately results in a decrease of information.* To help clarify this somewhat unusual notion, it is helpful to consider how the alphabet can be used to build up a language.[36] For this purpose, let us next introduce an additional concept of importance, namely, that we can classify communication systems roughly into three main categories: discrete, continuous, and mixed. A language consists of sequences of discrete symbols we call letters; Morse code consists of sequences of dashes and dots. Other forms of communication, however, such as paintings, photographs, or television images, are continuous. Superficially this would seem to be the case also with music. However, these continuous media are frequently converted into discrete systems, as with the half-tone reproductions of photographs and the symbolic representation of music via musical score. As Shannon and Weaver define it:[37] "A discrete channel will mean a system whereby a sequence of choices from a finite set of elementary symbols, $S_1 \ldots S_n$, can be transmitted from one point to another." Moreover, "It is not required that all possible sequences of the S_i be capable of transmission on the system, certain sequences only may be allowed." Thus, to return to our consideration of language, we have twenty-seven letters in the alphabet including the space. The simplest type of sentence might be constructed by selecting letters sequentially with the choice of letters being completely random, this choice being arrived at by assigning equal probabilities to each letter of the alphabet. The result bears little resemblance to an English sentence, however, except by pure chance. The situation is one of highest potential information content: *Anything might be said.* We can, however, reduce the information content of this random language in order to achieve some higher degree of "meaning" by altering the probabilities used to select the letters of the alphabet. Thus, we can first assign probabilities based on the frequencies with which letters occur in the English language. The next step beyond this is to assign probabilities based on the frequencies with which letters occur one after the other. In this way, freedom of choice is gradually reduced, and the results begin to take on a more and more recognizable form. The decrease in information which

---

[36] Shannon and Weaver, *op. cit.,* pp. 13–14.
[37] *Ibid.,* p. 7.

occurs is said to be the consequence of introducing *redundancy,* which is therefore related to order as information is related to disorder. This particular example of language construction, incidentally, is worked out in some detail by Shannon and Weaver.

"Information" is thus defined as the result of "choice" and is given a statistical significance based upon probability theory. It is possible, therefore, to write algebraic expressions for the information content of a communication system. In order to do this, the information content of the system is defined purely in terms of the number of possible choices inherent in the system itself. If we know nothing about the system, in other words, if we are unable to define any of its properties, we must assume that the choice is random, which is equivalent to saying that the information content of the system is at a maximum. On the other hand, if we happen to possess some information concerning the properties of the system, it is probable that we can restrict the choice process to a situation that is less than totally random. This means that the information content of the system has been reduced, or, in other words, we might state that the information we, as observers of the system, have acquired concerning its properties has been obtained at the expense of the information content of the system. The more information about the system we acquire, the less information the system contains. Therefore, according to Brillouin:[38]

. . . we consider a problem involving a certain number of possible answers, if we have no special information on the actual situation. When we happen to be in possession of some information on the problem, the number of possible answers is reduced, and complete information may even leave us with only one possible answer. Information is a function of the ratio of the number of possible answers before and after [a choice process], and we choose a logarithmic law in order to insure additivity of the information contained in independent situations.

We may now follow Brillouin[39] to define information algebraically:

Let us consider a situation in which P_0 different possible things might happen but with the condition that these P_0 possible outcomes are equally probable *a priori.* This is the initial situation, when we have no special information about the system under consideration. If we obtain more information about the problem, we may be able to specify that only one out of the P_0 outcomes is actually realized. *The greater the uncertainty in the initial problem is, the greater* P_0

[38] Brillouin, *op. cit.,* Introduction.
[39] *Ibid.,* pp. 1 ff.

will be, and the larger will be the amount of information required to make the selection. Summarizing, we have:

Initial situation: $I_0 = 0$ with P_0 equally probable outcomes;

Final situation: $I_1 \neq 0$, with $P_1 = 1$, i.e., one single outcome selected. The symbol I denotes information, and the definition of the information is

$$I_1 = K \ln P_0 \qquad (1)$$

where K is a constant and "ln" means the natural logarithm to the base e.

The definition of the measure of information can be generalized to cover the case when P_0 possibilities exist in the initial situation, while the final situation still contains P_1 possibilities;

Initially: $I_0 = 0$ with P_0 equally probable cases;

Finally: $I_1 \neq 0$ with P_1 equally probable cases.

In such a case we take

$$I_1 = K \ln (P_0/P_1) = K \ln P_0 - K \ln P_1 \qquad (2)$$

This definition reduces to Eq. 1 when $P_1 = 1$. [Italics supplied.]

The two cases discussed by Brillouin which apply to systems narrowed down to one choice in the first case and to a number of choices in the second case depend on the assumption of equal a priori probabilities. This is the simplest condition for, as we shall see, it is also possible to have unequal a priori probabilities, probabilities conditioned by previous choices and many more complex situations.

At this point, it is crucial to note that Equations (1) and (2) bear a striking resemblance to an equation, well known to physical scientists familiar with statistical mechanics, which relates thermodynamic probability and entropy. *Thermodynamic probability,* roughly, is a measure of the number of ways in which a physical system might be arranged, and *entropy* is related to this function by means of the following expression:

$$S = k \ln W \qquad (3)$$

where S is the entropy of the system, W is the thermodynamic probability, and k is Boltzmann's constant, equal to 1.36×10^{-16} erg/degree C. We may now relate information and entropy through the ratio k/K, the exact value of which depends on the units used to express information.

The question now arises as to the significance of the concept of entropy. It is essentially a measure of the degree of disorder or randomness in a physical system. Whenever a change occurs in some physical system which results in a decrease in order, the entropy of the system is said to increase. Conversely, an increase in order results in a decrease in entropy. For example, if a sample of crystalline ice is melted to form liquid water, there results an increase of entropy, because in the crystalline ice water molecules are arranged in a highly ordered lattice structure, while in liquid water these same molecules are more nearly scattered at random. Converting liquid water to steam involves yet another entropy gain, because this process causes the water molecules to become widely scattered and to move about at high velocity through a large volume of space. Scrambling an egg is an even simpler example of an entropy change. No chemical change occurs during this process, only mixing; however, after scrambling, because the resulting mixture is more random than before, the entropy content of the egg has increased. Even shuffling a sorted deck of cards can in a sense be said to bring about a change of entropy. It takes work to sort the cards into an ordered sequence, and this work can be thought of as an extraction of entropy. The problem of unscrambling an egg is also a problem involving the extraction of entropy.

In 1929, Szilard[40] recognized the close similarity between information and entropy, but the significance of this relationship was not generally recognized until it was rediscovered years later by Shannon to lead to the current development of information theory. It is now recognized that entropy is a measure of *missing information*. Thus, in the physical sciences, where all systems (except perfect crystals at absolute zero, $-273.16°C$) have positive entropy content, we find that all systems except these must of necessity be incompletely defined, this incompleteness being in direct relation to their entropy contents. To go back to our examples, we see that we know more about water molecules in crystalline ice than in liquid water, because, if for no other reason, we at least know more precisely where the molecules are.

We can now reproduce from Shannon and Weaver two useful propositions. Shannon and Weaver[41] note that the entropy of a communication system will be zero "if and only if all the P_i but one are zero, this one having the value unity. Thus, only when we are certain of the outcome does [the entropy] vanish. Otherwise [the entropy] is positive." Moreover, "for a given [number of possible choices], [the entropy] n is a maximum and equal to log n when all the P_i are equal, i.e., $1/n$. This is also intuitively the most uncertain situation." And lastly, "any change towards equalization of the probabilities, P_i, increases [the entropy]."

[40] L. Szilard, "Über die Entropieverminderung in einem thermodynamischen System bei Eingriffen intelligenter Wesen," Z. Physik, 53:840, 1929.
[41] Shannon and Weaver, op. cit., p. 21.

The definition of information as a measure of a number of choices from a random arrangement of a finite set of elements is unquestionably confusing when first met with, so it is important that it be clearly understood that by "information" we do *not* mean information in the everyday sense. "Information" in information theory is *not* the same thing as "meaning," particularly semantic meaning, or "specific knowledge about," which are definitions more nearly synonymous with the common use of the word. To clarify this point, Weaver states that:[42] "The word information in communication theory relates not so much to what you *do* say as to what you *could* say. . . . The concept of information applies not to the individual messages (as the concept of meaning would) but rather to the situation as a whole."

In a similar vein, Brillouin concludes:[39]

Our definition of information is an absolute objective definition, independent of the observer. . . . The restrictions we have introduced enable us to give a quantitative definition of information and to treat information as a physically measurable quantity. . . . We define "information" as distinct from "knowledge" for which we have no numerical measure. . . .

Moreover, as Weaver points out:[43]

The concept of information developed in this theory at first seems disappointing and bizarre—disappointing because it has nothing to do with meaning, and bizarre because it deals not with a single message but rather with the statistical character of a whole ensemble of messages, bizarre also because in these statistical terms the two words *information* and *uncertainty* find themselves to be partners.

However, Weaver suggests that: "one is now, perhaps, for the first time, ready for a real theory of meaning." He attempts to set up this problem for future study by suggesting "three levels of communication," namely:[44]

Level A. How accurately can the symbols of communication be transmitted? (The technical problem.)

Level B. How precisely do the transmitted symbols convey the desired meaning? (The semantic problem.)

Level C. How effectively does the received meaning affect conduct in the desired way? (The effectiveness problem.)

[42] *Ibid.*, p. 110.
[43] *Ibid.*, p. 116.
[44] *Ibid.*, pp. 95–96.

In this connection, it has been stressed by Weaver that there may be a high degree of overlap between the three levels. He suggests that:[45]

A larger part of the significance [of information theory] comes from the fact that the analysis at level A discloses that this level overlaps the other levels more than one could possibly naively suspect. Thus, the theory of level A is, at least to a significant degree, also the theory of levels B and C.

Brillouin similarly recognizes two areas of investigation which lie outside current research in information theory. He points out[46] that the next problem to be defined is the problem of semantic information, i.e., whether or not a message makes sense. As noted by Brillouin, some exploratory investigations of this problem in language have apparently been carried out by Ville[47] and by Carnap and Bar-Hillel,[48] who based their work on the methods of symbolic logic, but this seems to be about the extent of current research in this area. Lastly, Brillouin recognizes the problem of "value," i.e., whether or not the message is of value to the sender or receiver. Here, he says we "invade a territory reserved for philosophy. . . . Shall we ever be able to cross this border? . . . This is for the future to decide." This is, of course, Weaver's level C, which in his estimation involves aesthetic considerations in the fine arts.[49]

To summarize: (1) in recent years, information theory has been applied to certain practical problems of communication engineering.[50] (2) Certain authors have suggested that the concepts of information theory might well be used more generally than just in engineering problems. (3) *Information* is defined as proportional to the logarithm of the number of possible choices available when making a decision. Information is thus analogous to entropy. (4) Inasmuch as common communication systems utilize finite sets of discrete symbols, these symbols can be selected sequentially by what we will call a *stochastic process* to build up a "message." The information,

---

[45] Ibid., p. 98.

[46] Brillouin, *op. cit.*, pp. 297 ff.

[47] J. Ville, *Actualitiés sci. et ind.*, 1145:101–114, Hermann, Paris, 1951.

[48] Y. Bar-Hillel and R. Carnap, "Semantic Information," *Brit. J. Phil. Sci.*, 4:147, 1953; see also C. Cherry, *On Human Communication*, John Wiley & Sons, Inc., New York, 1957, pp. 231–250, for a detailed discussion of this problem based on another paper by these same authors, namely: R. Carnap and Y. Bar-Hillel, "An Outline of a Theory of Semantic Information," *M.I.T., Research Lab. Electronics Tech. Rept. 247*, 1953.

[49] Shannon and Weaver, *op. cit.*, p. 97.

[50] In fact, it might be of interest to note that these applications have now become sufficiently extensive that a technical journal, *IRE Transactions on Information Theory*, which is devoted specifically to this subject, is now being published.

or entropy, content of a communication system is at a maximum if there are the least number of restrictions upon the process of selecting successive events; specifically, the largest entropy content is obtained whenever the sequence of symbols is completely random.

Information Theory and Music

It is now necessary to examine how these concepts relate to the definitions of musical meaning and form previously discussed. We can start by noting that not only has Weaver suggested in general terms that information theory can be applied to the study of art, but that Pinkerton,[51] for example, has proposed that the theory might be used in studies of music. Also, fairly ambitious theoretical attempts to apply information theory to the study of music have been published by W. Meyer-Eppler[52] and A. Moles.[53] Moreover, Leonard Meyer, whose concepts were reviewed in some detail earlier in this chapter, has also recently recognized many corresponding properties between his theories of musical meaning and information theory.[54] Thus, Meyer acknowledges the equivalence between his ideas of ambiguity and precision of form and entropy variation and, secondly, the importance of sequential choice processes in the building up of musical structures.

Some main points of Moles' applications of information theory to musical communication can now be summarized. Moles postulates two determining factors which permit a listener to build messages out of musical sounds, namely, *memory* and *attention,* i.e., perception. This is, of course, in accord with traditional aesthetic theory. Moles then notes that memory appears to be divided, in terms of span, into three categories: (1) instantaneous memory, (2) dated memory, and (3) undated memorization. However, it is to the problem of attention that he has directed most of his studies. He suggests that "attention" can be divided into two distinct "modes": (1)

---

[51] R. C. Pinkerton, "Information Theory and Melody," *Sci. American,* 194(2):77, February, 1956.

[52] W. Meyer-Eppler, "Statistic and Psychologic Problems of Sound," *Die Reihe,* 1:55 ff.; "Informationstheorie," *Naturwissenschaften,* 39:341, 1952. A review of some of Meyer-Eppler's views is also given in an article by H. Le Caine, "Electronic Music," *Proc. I.R.E.,* 44:457, 1956.

[53] A. Moles, "Informationstheorie der Musik," *Nachr. Technik Fachberichte,* 3:47, 1956; *Théorie de l'Information et perception esthétique,* Presses Universitaires de France, Paris, 1957; *Some Basic Aspects of an Informational Theory of Music,* unpublished manuscript; and other writings. Also private conversations between Dr. Moles and one of the present authors (L. A. H.) in Paris, June, 1957.

[54] L. B. Meyer, "Meaning in Music and Information Theory, *J. of Aesthetics and Art Criticism,* 15:412, 1957.

the *semantic mode* and (2) the *aesthetic mode*. The semantic mode is characterized as the "language side of music—a system of organized and standardized symbols—which can be *coded* [55]—i.e., translated into another language—the *score*." On the other hand, the aesthetic mode "does not appeal to intellectual faculties, but to the directly sensorial ones—even sensual at the limit." Moles thus differentiates two types of structures as does Tischler[18] and defines the term *acoustical quanta*. These quanta "make up the repertory of aesthetic symbols at a given scale of duration [and] information rate, H_e,—[which] can then be computed and which comes parallel to the semantic information rate, H_s." Moles' purpose is "to study the properties of the aesthetic message—*vs.* the semantic one, both being bound into the same sequence of acoustical sets of quanta grasped in a different manner."

One additional point made by Moles is of interest:

The fact acknowledged by many psychologists dealing with the human operator that one is unable to grasp a message of more than 10–20 bits/second,[56] compared with the estimated maximal capacity of some hundred bits/second) implies that perception is a selection of definite symbols in the whole of the message and that these symbols, these Gestalt are not picked at random, which would simply express the utter incapacity of the listener to cope with a too original message.[57] In consequence, the structure of Music itself regarding the color, thickness and rate of originality of the musical stuff should be directly considered by the composer. This leads to the concept of "authentic composition" (Meyer-Eppler) which has recently found its way into experimental music.

The first point to decide, if practical musical applications are to be made for the concepts of information theory, is whether music is basically a discrete, a continuous, or a mixed communication system. We should like to propose that it is effectively a discrete system. It is thus like language, although normally more complex operationally, because in language only one symbol for an operational element is considered at a time. In music, a number of elements are normally in operation simultaneously.

There are a variety of ways in which music operates through discrete elements. Most importantly, as Helmholtz, for example, has noted:[58]

---

[55] The idea of coding is considered in Chapter 4 in relation to computer operation.
[56] A *bit* is a unit quantity of information and is a term used in digital-computer theory. See Chapter 4.
[57] I.e., a message with too high an entropy content.
[58] Helmholtz, *op. cit.*, pp. 250–253.

Alterations of pitch in melodies take place by intervals and not by continuous transitions. The psychological basis of this fact would seem to be the same as that which led to rhythmic subdivision periodically repeated. . . . The musical scale is as it were the divided rod, by which we measure progression in pitch, as rhythm measures progression in time. Hence, the analogy between the scale of tones and rhythm occurred to musical theoreticians of ancient as well as modern times.

We consequently find the most complete agreement among all nations that use music at all, from the earliest to the latest times, as to the separation of certain determinate degrees of tone from the possible mass of continuous gradations of sound, all of which are audible, and these degrees form the scale in which the melody moves. But in selecting the particular degrees of pitch, deviations of national taste become immediately apparent. The number of scales used by different nations and at different times is by no means small.

Almost all music notation, in fact, is based upon a definition of discrete musical elements. Thus, except possibly for such recent artifacts as some forms of electronic music (Chapter 3), we can define the basic texture of music as an assembly of discrete symbols with the few exceptions (such as continuous dynamics changes) being so simple that these are readily taken care of independently.

Secondly, restricting the number of choices should tend to increase the "meaningfulness" of messages. Thus, the most diffuse type of music is produced on the average when successive note selection is permitted to be completely random. As we shall see, music of this type is rather easily generated in a computer and *forms the basic substance from which we must fashion more characteristic structures.* Thus, we note that our operational basis is entirely in accord with Stravinsky's concepts of the logic of musical composition discussed earlier in this chapter. Or, as noted by Helmholtz:[59] "Music alone finds an infinitely rich but totally shapeless plastic material in the tone of the human voice and artificial musical instruments which must be shaped on purely artistic principles."

Thirdly, the problem arises as to what techniques to apply to restrict successive choices if we desire to produce music less chaotic than random music. It is possible, for example, to apply statistical methods and compute transition probabilities for successive note selection based upon the analysis of some known species of music. Pinkerton worked out a simple example of how this can be done by constructing a transition-probabilities table based upon the analysis of a set of nursery tunes. Pinkerton quite cor-

[59] *Ibid.,* p. 250.

rectly observed, however, that the use of such tables leads to the construction of "banal" tunes as a general rule. It is easy to see that this is bound to occur whenever a purely statistical analysis to determine mean choices is used as an aesthetic basis for computing transition probabilities. The difficulty here is an aesthetic one; if we wish to generate something besides banal music, other criteria must be sought.

In this connection, we should mention also that a similar but more thorough study has been carried out recently by Brooks, Hopkins, Neumann, and Wright,[60] to whom we refer also in Chapter 3, since these authors coded their ideas for computer processing. Like Pinkerton, these authors subjected a sampling of simple tunes (this time hymn tunes) to statistical analysis to form transition-probability tables. However, their analysis was more elegant, since they carried out their calculations to the extent of eighth-order probabilities, i.e., to include into the calculations relationships as far as eight notes back. On the other hand, there is considerable danger in elaborating a simple eighth-order process to produce music, since aside from simple tunes such as hymn tunes, there is little music in which a fluctuation of transition probabilities from one part of a composition to another would not occur. This danger has been recognized, incidentally, by Meyer.[54] Consequently, means are required for controlling fluctuations between randomness and order during the course of a composition.

Still another study in this same vein has been recently published by Youngblood.[61] In contrast to the above studies, Youngblood has computed sets of transition probabilities derived from the analysis of fairly complex art music. For his study, Youngblood has chosen a group of songs by Schubert, Mendelssohn, and Schumann and has compared the results obtained from the music of these three composers. He has tabulated differences as reflected in transition probabilities and information contents between the individual styles of these composers, as well as similarities which one would, of course, expect, since all three employ the same basic style of composition.

Lastly, two other recent incidents of rather simple applications of the idea of sequential-choice processes to compose music have been also reported by J. R. Pierce.[62] Thus:

[60] F. P. Brooks, Jr., A. L. Hopkins, Jr., P. G. Neumann, and W. V. Wright, "An Experiment in Musical Composition," *IRE Trans. on Electronic Computers*, EC-6:175, 1957.

[61] J. E. Youngblood, "Style as Information," *J. of Music Theory*, 2:24, 1958.

[62] J. R. Pierce, letter to *Sci. American*, 194(4):18, April, 1956.

J. J. Coupling has discussed stochastic composition of music in "Science for Art's Sake" in *Astounding Science Fiction*, Nov., 1950. [Similarly] Dr. D. Slepian of Bell experimented with stochastic composition, not using statistics but such ideas of probability as have accumulated in the minds of a group of experimenters. Thus, he had each of a group of men add to a "composition" after examining only one or more preceding half measures. Tape recordings of the resulting music have been played as a part of a number of talks on information theory.

Pierce himself, in collaboration with M. E. Shannon, has also worked out an example of stochastic music, this music involving common chords selected in random sequences. This particular example of stochastic music is reproduced in a recent book by Pierce.[62a]

It can be seen that the various experiments to produce stochastic music thus far carried out are subject to critical limitations of one type or another. The end products, if not banal, as Pinkerton termed his results, nevertheless remain rather primitive. In designing our experiments, we were well aware of the difficulty of basing experiments utilizing these new techniques on initial operating principles which might appear on first inspection to be far removed from traditional musical procedures. An alternative procedure was to combine relevant concepts of traditional musical experience with the operating techniques derived from information theory and to take advantage of Weaver's suggestion that there is extensive overlap between the three areas of investigation relevant to information theory. In this way, we would use the stimulus provided by working with traditional music concepts in terms of new operational principles as a point of departure for formulating abstract structural bases for music synthesis.

It is interesting to note, in concluding, that attempts to apply information theory to musical problems raise in a new guise an old issue which has been a source of dispute in musical aesthetics many times in the past. It is yet another attempt to codify musical aesthetics in terms of natural law. This is, of course, an argument resorted to by many writers ever since music was defined as an imitation of nature in ancient times. Zarlino, for example, looked "on music as an imitation of nature and endeavored to derive his teachings from natural law," [63] i.e., in accord with Pythagorean and Platonic theory. On the other hand, Vincenzo Galilei in attacking Zarlino's teachings "considered numerical ratios irrelevant to the artist and the rules

[62a] J. R. Pierce, *Electrons, Waves and Messages*, Hanover House, Garden City, N.Y., 1956, pp. 271–274.

[63] O. Strunk, *Source Readings in Music History*, W. W. Norton & Company, Inc., New York, 1959, p. 228.

of counterpoint a product of the demands of taste, experience and aesthetic purpose." [64] More recently Helmholtz remarked that: [65]

. . . to furnish a satisfactory foundation for the elementary rules of musical composition . . . we tread on new ground, which is no longer subject to physical laws alone. . . . Hence it follows—*that the system of Scales, Modes, and Harmonic Tissues does not rest solely upon inalterable natural laws, but is also, at least partly, the result of aesthetical principles, which have already changed, and will still further change, with the progressive development of humanity.* [Helmholtz's italics.]

A more subtle statement of the same basic thesis is contained in Meyer's recent book, already referred to, when he remarks[66] that three interrelated errors have continually plagued music theory, namely, *hedonism,* the philosophy that pleasure is the primary purpose of musical experience; *atomism,* which is the attempt to characterize music solely by means of its discrete elements; and *universalism,* which is "the belief that the responses obtained by experiment or otherwise are universal, natural, and necessary. This universalist approach is also related to the time-honored search for a physical quasi-acoustical explanation of musical experience—the attempt, that is, to account for musical communication in terms of vibration ratios of intervals, and the like." What effect information theory will have on this problem will be of considerable interest to watch in the future.

To summarize, music, being a nondiscursive form of communication, operates with a semantic peculiarly dependent upon technical structure as such. Therefore, the study of musical structure in terms of information theory should be a significant technique for breaking through the "semantic barrier" which seems to hamper current investigations in information theory and should perhaps also lead to an improved delineation of the aesthetic basis of musical composition. Specifically, in light of the apparent close dependence of meaning upon form in music, we suggest that Weaver's overlap, if it exists, is particularly significant in music. The aesthetic significance, or "value," of a musical composition depends in considerable measure upon its relationship to our inner mental and emotional transitions, but this relationship is largely perceived in music through the articulation of musical forms. The articulation of musical forms can be considered the semantic content of music, and this in turn can best be understood in terms of the technical problems of musical composition. Since the articulation of

[64] Palisca, *op. cit.*
[65] Helmholtz, *op. cit.*, pp. 250–251.
[66] Meyer, *op. cit.*, p. 5.

musical forms is the primary problem faced by composers, it seemed most logical to start our investigation by attempting first to restate the techniques used by composers in terms both compatible with information theory and translatable into computer programs utilizing sequential-choice operations as a basis for music generation. In our investigation, as we have already noted, therefore, we first studied the traditional craft acquired by every composer, namely, counterpoint, harmony, rhythm, melodic construction, and similar basic problems. Only after results were achieved in this investigation did we feel that we could apply more experimental processes. Not unexpectedly, work of this nature soon led to speculation as to whether there exist more general principles of musical composition suitable for computer use. It is seen that in this approach we used the differentiation of internal and external relations suggested by Tischler, or alternately, the distinction between semantic and aesthetic quanta as suggested by Moles as a basic operating premise. However, we did not feel that the closer dependence of the relevant external meanings upon internal musical relationships suggested by Meyer conflicted with this experimental approach, since Meyer's analysis of musical meaning represents a broadening of these concepts rather than a departure from them.

CHAPTER THREE

Experimental Music

Experimental Music Defined

It is the purpose of this chapter to summarize recent technical and artistic developments relevant to the subject of modern experimental electronic and synthetic music. Our primary purpose is to show how the present study of computer-produced music is related to and yet distinguished from other recent experiments in the production of music by unusual means. It is our understanding that this general subject, including even a brief discussion of our work based upon a limited amount of information, has been recently reviewed in considerable detail in an as yet unpublished treatise by Abraham Moles,[1] presently associated with the *Centre d'Études Radiophoniques* in Paris, one of the several European groups currently working in this general area. An introductory review of the topic of recent electronic music experiments is contained in two recent articles published in *The Reporter*.[2] Moreover, V. Ussachevsky[3] has written just recently a review article sur-

---

[1] A. Moles, *Experimental Music*, in manuscript.

[2] R. Maren, "Music by Montage and Mixing," *The Reporter*, 13(5):38, Oct. 6, 1955; R. Maren, "Electronic Music: Untouched by Human Hands," *ibid.*, 16(8):40, April 18, 1957.

[3] V. Ussachevsky, "The Processes of Experimental Music," *J. Audio Engineering Soc.*, in press.

veying the current status of European experimentation. Lastly, Le Caine[4] has written an informative historical survey of the subject of both electronic instruments and of recent experiments in coded electronic music.

In considering this subject ourselves, we shall limit our discussion arbitrarily to novel *means of composition and sound production,* and, moreover, we will stress the difference between attempts at rationalization of the laws of musical composition and attempts to substitute and make use of modern means of sound production to produce an aural effect. Thus, we will immediately exclude from consideration forms of composition involving either a composer writing music on paper in the traditional sense or experimentation with novel sound effects and timbres utilizing conventional musical instruments. In so doing, we are, of course, not at all implying that significant new music is not being written by these more traditional procedures; we are simply restricting our discussion to the most directly related material. Secondly, given this restriction of subject matter, it seems convenient to classify current research in experimental music into two basic categories: (1) We can group together *experimental studies of the logic of musical composition.* In terms of most recent work, this would refer most specifically to the use of automatic high-speed digital computers to produce musical output. For convenience, we may term such music *computational music,* in general, and the specific type produced with computers, *computer music.* (2) We can consider experiments involving primarily *the production of musical sounds by means other than the use of conventional instruments played by performers.* In this category, we refer to the production of musical sounds by electronic means and by the manipulation of magnetic recording tape in tape recorders and related devices. For our purposes, it is convenient to group all these experiments under the name of *electronic,* or *synthetic, music,* though in so doing, we refer to a broader body of work than just the *elektronische musik* produced at present in Cologne, Germany. In this second group of experiments, principles have had to be formulated for "composing" as well as for the actual technical production of sound, but the choice process for selecting materials to go into a "composition" is still carried out entirely by the "composer." It is seen that the two types of experiments are complimentary rather than competitive. In fact, there are a number of ways in which the results of the two types of experimentation might be used in the future to enhance the effectiveness of each. This we shall consider in Chapter 7.

[4] H. Le Caine, "Electronic Music," *Proc. I.R.E.,* 44:457, 1956.

Electronic, or Synthetic, Music

Up until the end of World War II, the applications of electronic circuits to the production of musical sounds had been largely restricted to the design and development of a number of practical musical instruments intended for live performance. Excluding from consideration the use of amplifiers to enlarge the sound of conventional musical instruments such as guitars, these *electrophones,* as they are defined by Curt Sachs,[5] seem conveniently to be divided into two groups of instruments. The first group includes the well-known commercial electronic organs such as the Hammond and Baldwin. The primary purpose of these instruments is to provide a facsimile of pipe-organ sound rather than to provide a fundamentally new musical timbre. The technical details of how these instruments operate are quite interesting, however, and can be found in the literature.[6]

Of somewhat greater interest have been several more novel electrophones, such as the Theremin, or Etherophone, invented by L. Theremin in 1924, Les ondes musicales, or Les ondes Martenot, invented by M. Martenot, also in 1924, and a number of more recent instruments, such as the Mixturtrautonium, invented in 1930 and refined by Oskar Sala. Most of these instruments are monophonic rather than polyphonic devices. The Hammond Solovox attachment perhaps also falls into this group. All are designed to supplement conventional instrumental groups and are, therefore, new additions to the standard body of musical instruments. These instruments are designed for live performance and do not represent a basic departure in performance practice. However, these instruments do produce new instrumental timbres which have been exploited to a limited extent by contemporary composers, particularly in France.[7] Recently, for example,

[5] C. Sachs, *The History of Musical Instruments,* W. W. Norton & Company, Inc., New York, 1940, pp. 447–449.

[6] R. H. Dorf, *Electronic Musical Instruments,* Radio Magazine, Inc., Mineola, N.Y., 1954; A. Douglas, *The Electronic Music Instrument Manual,* 3d ed., Sir Isaac Pitman and Sons, Ltd., London, 1957; E. G. Richardson, "Electrophonic Instruments," in E. Blom (ed.), *Grove's Dictionary of Music and Musicians,* 5th ed., The Macmillan Company, New York, 1954, vol. II, pp. 905–908. It should be noted that Dorf's book contains an extensive bibliography and patent list.

[7] For example, several works by Oliver Messiaen, including *Fête des Belles Eaux,* 1938, for six ondes Martenot and *Trois Petites Liturgies de la Présence Divine,* 1944, for unison soprano choir, celesta, vibraphone, maracas, Chinese cymbals, gong, pianoforte, ondes Martenot, and strings. Also, André Jolivet has written a *Concerto for Ondes Martenot and Orchestra,* 1947, which has recently been recorded on Westminster XWN 18360.

Les ondes Martenot and the Mixturtrautonium were featured instruments at the 1st International Congress of Electronic Music and Musique Concrète at Basel, Switzerland.[8] Detailed descriptions of these instruments are given in the literature references already cited.[4, 6] The "electronic sackbut" designed by Le Caine since 1945 should also be mentioned, particularly since the sounds produced by this instrument are rather strikingly different from those produced by most of the instruments just mentioned.[4] Most monophonic electronic instruments happen to be modified audio oscillators and the most usual tone color they produce is simple sine-wave sound; i.e., pure harmonic sound consisting solely of a fundamental free of overtones.

A second technical achievement of major consequence, realized around the end of World War II, was the commercial production of high-fidelity magnetic tape recorders. With these instruments, for the first time, it has become possible to record music—or for that matter, sounds of any sort— easily, accurately, and at reasonable cost. Secondly, and of equal importance, it has become possible with these instruments to edit and to alter the sounds once they are recorded. While it had been possible to produce, previously, fine recordings by means of disc recording, it was also true that adequate equipment for this purpose was expensive and elaborate. Noncommercial disc recording was inherently unsatisfactory. Moreover, editing and alteration of the recorded sounds were entirely impractical.

Once tape recorders became available, it was not long before their possibilities for musical "composition" were recognized. Apparently, among the first to experiment with tape recorders to produce a new type music was Pierre Schaeffer, whose initial work around 1948 has led to the development of what is now termed *musique concrète.* This is the first of several types of synthetic music which we shall now briefly review. Since our discussion of this subject is meant to be illustrative rather than exhaustive, only the most important of these studies will be mentioned.

Musique Concrète. This name is given to the musical products of a group directed by Pierre Schaeffer working for Radiodiffusion Française. In producing *musique concrète,* a point is made on certain obscure aesthetic grounds of utilizing only sounds which originate in "nature"—in other words, sounds produced by electronic means are excluded from consideration. These "natural" sounds, however, are subjected to considerable alteration during the course of "composition" by means of several simple but efficient pieces of equipment. The best known of these is the Phonogène, designed by Pierre Schaeffer, which permits direct transposition by means

[8] Anon., *Time,* 65(23):78, June 6, 1955.

of independently operated tape travelers of tape-recorded material to twelve different pitches. Equipment for synthetic reverberation, montaging, and variable speed control is also available.

In addition to Pierre Schaeffer, the principal composer within the *musique concrète* group is Pierre Henry. From time to time, however, other composers including Milhaud, Varese, and Messiaen have used their facilities. A two-record set of recording of *musique concrète* is available in this country.[9] Included in the records is one particularly striking piece of music, *Le Voile d'Orphée,* by Pierre Henry.

At the present time, the principal research objectives of the *musique concrète* group appear to be (1) the development of a notation for their music, since up to this point the selection of materials for compositions has been entirely empirical, and (2) the application of *musique concrète* to radio, television, movies, and the theater. No major expansion of their technical resources is apparently contemplated at the present time.

There is a growing literature on the subject. Perhaps the best sources of information at the present time are a short mimeographed book issued by the group which reviews their work through 1955,[10] and a recent special issue of *La Revue Musicale.*[11]

A bibliography of publications concerned with *musique concrète* is included in the house publication referred to.[8] There are also brief discussions of *musique concrète* available in publications in English.[12]

Elektronische Musik. A second and somewhat competitive European development is the *elektronische musik* prepared at the N.W.D.R. broadcasting studios in Cologne, Germany. This laboratory for experimental electronic music was started by Herbert Eimert, its present director, and Werner Meyer-Eppler in the period following World War II. While there are only two "staff composers," namely, Karlheinz Stockhausen and G. M. Koenig, employed by the studio, other composers such as Ernst Krenek and Pierre Boulez have used their facilities to produce *elektronische musik* compositions.

[9] P. Schaeffer, P. Henry, P. Arthuys, and M. Phillipot, *Panorama of Musique Concrète,* vol. I, London DTL 93090, vol. II, London DTL 93121.

[10] Radiodiffusion-Television Française, Groupe de Recherches de Musique Concrète, *Sept Ans de Musique Concrète,* 1948–1955, Centre d'Études Radiophoniques, Paris.

[11] "Vers une Musique Expérimentale—sous la Direction de Pierre Schaeffer," *La Revue Musicale,* numero spéciale 236, 1957.

[12] H. Searle, "Concrete Music," in E. Blom (ed.), *Grove's Dictionary of Music and Musicians,* 5th ed., The Macmillan Company, New York, 1954, vol. IX, app. II, pp. 571–572; R. S. Brindle, "The Lunatic Fringe—I. Concrete Music," *The Musical Times,* 97:246, 1956.

The efforts of this group have been widely publicized, and information concerning their activities is readily available in both German and English. Besides various reviews and critical articles in various German music journals,[13] authoritative statements from this studio are contained in a publication called *Die Reihe,* distributed by Universal Edition, Vienna. Volume 1 of this journal is devoted exclusively to articles on the Cologne experiments. This apparently will be the case also with volume 3, which we have not yet seen, while volume 2 contains articles about Anton Webern, with whom the Cologne experimenters claim close artistic affinity. Volumes 1 and 2 have also been made available in this country in English translation by the Theodore Presser Company. Also in English, there exists a rather extensive informal description of the activities of this studio by Allen Forte,[14] and a number of shorter articles can be cited.[15]

In preparing *elektronische musik,* in contrast to *musique concrète,* synthetic sound sources are used. According to Forte,[14] there are a number of these in the Cologne studio, including a Bode-Melochord—an electronic instrument with two organlike keyboards; a Monochord—not the classic monochord, but rather a device which can produce two tones at once and also provides for continuous variation of frequency for *glissando*-type effects; a noise generator; a buzzer; and a tone or frequency generator. This last, in particular, seems to be the favored device because of the aesthetic significance this group attaches to simple sine waves. Output from these various units is recorded on magnetic tape for storage and for subsequent processing basically similar to that employed to produce *musique concrète.* In other words, the usual techniques of reverberation, variation of the frequency and amplitude of the sound, montage, and so on are employed to build up a finished piece of music.

Compositions are planned by means of a special type of score notation,

[13] For example, R. Sonner, "Elektronische Musik," *Z. für Musik,* 116:449, 1955; R. Beyer, "Zur Situation der Elektronischen Musik," *ibid.,* 452; A. L. Sieder, "Die überflüssige Windmaschine," *ibid.,* 456. Recent issues of *Melos Magazine,* published by Der Melos Verlag, Mainz, Germany, also contain numerous articles on electronic music and related topics.

[14] A. Forte, "Composing with Electrons at Cologne," *High Fidelity,* 6(10):64, October, 1956.

[15] E. Krenek, "New Development in Electronic Music," *Musical America,* 75(11):8, September, 1955; R. S. Brindle, "The Lunatic Fringe—II. Electronic Music," *The Musical Times,* 97:300, 1956; R. Vlad, "Die Reihe and Electronic Music," *The Score,* 13:23, 1955; H. Searle, "Electrophonic Music," in E. Blom (ed.), *Grove's Dictionary of Music and Musicians,* 5th ed., The Macmillan Company, New York, 1954, vol. IX, app. II, p. 573.

a sample of which is reprinted in *Die Reihe*.[16] A compositional aesthetic for planning the scores of these works has also been evolved. This aesthetic is rather loosely derived from twelve-tone-row techniques, although this music is, of course, not limited to the usual even-tempered scale. Indeed, a direct evolution from Webern's compositional techniques is postulated. Serial techniques and number sequences are employed to control pitch, tone duration, silences, and intensities of the musical elements employed in a composition. Following an initial broadcast of seven compositions in October, 1954, a number of compositions by Stockhausen and other composers have been presented publicly at various contemporary music festivals in Europe such as at Darmstadt, Germany. Commercial recordings of some of these pieces have been released by Deutsches Grammophon in Europe and are now available in this country through Theodore Presser.[17] Until recently, the only way to hear this music in this country had been via privately owned tapes brought back from Germany by various people interested in electronic music.

In contrast to *musique concrète,* much of *elektronische musik* sounds simple and almost primitive. Simple sine-wave tones, relative to which the most familiar instrumental equivalent is the recorder, lack harmonics and are, of course, neutral and unexciting in effect. Thus, even though this music is rather elaborately planned out, the over-all effect in the average *elektronische musik* composition, in which sine tones make up a relatively large proportion of the total sound, is curiously one of relative simplicity. However, more recently, experiments have also been carried out to combine the sounds of *elektronische musik* with processed sounds of recorded human voices to synthesize a cantata-like product. At least two such pieces have been produced, a cantata by Ernst Krenek and the *Song of the Holy Children* by Stockhausen. Here, as might be expected, the superposition of human voices upon the purely synthetic materials produces a more dramatic effect.

Other European Experimental Music. In Milan, Italy, a laboratory has also been set up by a broadcasting organization, the RAI Studio di Fonologìa Musicale, under the direction of Luciano Berio. In this studio, elements of both *musique concrète* and *elektronische musik* are being utilized to produce synthetic music utilizing sounds from both natural sources and from electronic sound-producing devices. A brief general description of the

[16] *Die Reihe,* vol. 1, facing p. 50 in English edition.
[17] H. Eimert, *Etude über Tongemische; Fünf Stücke; Glockenspiel,* DG–16132; K. Stockhausen, *Studie I; Studie II; Gesang der Junglinge.* DG–16133.

aims of this organization has been published by Berio.[18] To date, however, the activities of this group have not been publicized to an extent comparable to that of the older organizations.

A number of other laboratories are also springing up in Germany, in the Netherlands, and elsewhere in Europe, which more or less duplicate the facilities of those already described without thus far disclosing significantly different or startling advances in technique. A typical example is the experimental studio at Philips Research Laboratories at Eindhoven, The Netherlands.[19] These facilities have been employed by the composer Henk Badings to produce a twenty-minute score for a ballet entitled *Cain and Abel.*

American Experiments in Tape-recorder Music. A number of American composers have also examined the possibility of producing musical structures by electronic means and by processing tape-recorded sound materials. A review of earlier developments in this area in the United States has been written by Vladimir Ussachevsky,[20] who, in collaboration with Otto Luening, is perhaps the best-known experimentalist in this field in the United States. Using fairly simple equipment, these composers have thus far achieved types of sound synthesis similar to the European experiments. They have also been able to make some of their results available through recently released recordings.[21] In addition to demonstrating the effectiveness of this medium for purely abstract compositions, the value of tape-recorder music for theatrical purposes is disclosed in the *Suite from King Lear,* a set of examples of music used for Orson Welles's production of *King Lear* in New York in 1956.

Luening and Ussachevsky have been also concerned with the possibility of combining musical materials on tape with live performance; in other words, of writing compositions for tape recorder and other instruments. Luening's *Theater Piece No. 2,* which received its first performance in New York on April 20, 1956, combines tape recorder, voices, and chamber orchestra, while Luening and Ussachevsky, as a result of a commission,

[18] L. Berio, "Studio di Fonologìa Musicale," *The Score,* 15:83, 1955.
[19] H. Badings and J. W. de Bruyn, "Electronic Music," *Philips Tech. Rev.* 19:190, 1957–1958.
[20] V. Ussachevsky, "La 'Tape Music' aux États-Unis," *La Revue Musicale,* numero spéciale 236, p. 50, 1957.
[21] O. Luening and V. Ussachevsky, *Tape-recorder Music,* Innovations GB–1; O. Luening and V. Ussachevsky, *Rhapsodic Variations for Tape Recorder and Orchestra,* Columbia Records, Louisville series; O. Luening and V. Ussachevsky, *A Poem of Cycles and Bells, for Tape Recorder and Orchestra; Suite from King Lear;* V. Ussachevsky, *Piece for Tape Recorder,* Composers Recordings, Inc., CRI–112.

have written pieces for the Louisville and Los Angeles Philharmonic Orchestras.

Ussachevsky[20] reviews other American experiments up to 1953 as well as his own efforts. This includes early experiments of John Cage and his group involving the use of multichannel tape music to produce stereophonic effects.

There have been other experiments in this country which should also be mentioned. Notably, Edgar Varese has written a piece entitled *Deserts* for tape recorder and chamber orchestra, in which sound effects in nature are contrasted to orchestral sonorities[12] and more recently, *Poème Électronique* for Le Corbusier's Pavilion at the 1958 Brussels Exposition. Louis and Bebe Barron have prepared the sound track for an MGM science-fiction movie called *Forbidden Planet* through producing by electronic means upon magnetic tape what they have called *electronic tonalities.*[22]

Lastly, a rather different type of tape music might be mentioned, which is reminiscent of experiments carried out in the 1940s at Princeton University[23] and more recently for the National Film Board of Canada by McLaren[24] and by Kendall,[25] of marking film sound tracks directly with a stylus to produce sound patterns. This is the following:[26]

A. H. Frisch, of New York, is now working on a mechanical means of recording pitch and dynamics directly on tape. He is laying the basis for musical composition without recourse to any instruments. The composer will work with unmagnetized tape while sitting at his desk, and by applying to the tape specific *magnetic dyes* will transfer pitch or a theme from his creative innards to the tape. . . . He will also have a means of applying amplitude or dynamics or even vibrato. He will establish rhythm or timing by a preselected formula shown as specific intervals on a sort of yardstick over which the tape is manipulated, inch by inch, foot by foot.

The RCA Electronic Music Synthesizer. One of the most ambitious projects for the direct production of musical sound has been the construction of the RCA Electronic Music Synthesizer by H. Olson and H. Belar[27] at the

[22] L. and B. Barron, "Forbidden Planet," *Film Music*, 15(5):18, Summer, 1956.
[23] M. Babbitt, private communication.
[24] R. E. Lewis and N. McLaren, "Synthetic Sound on Film," *J. Soc. Motion Picture Engrs.*, 50:233, 1948.
[25] A. Phillips, "Osmond Kendall's Marvellous Music Machine," *MacLean's Magazine*, June 11, 1955, p. 22.
[26] S. J. White, Letter to the Editor, *High Fidelity*, 7(1):15, January, 1957.
[27] H. F. Olson and H. Belar, "Electronic Music Synthesizer," *J. Acoust. Soc. Am.*, 27:595, 1955.

RCA acoustics laboratories in Princeton, New Jersey. The Music Synthesizer is an elaborate electronic device controlled by means of coded paper input tape. The instrument builds up sounds by wave superposition and wave-form control to simulate known instrumental or even primitive vocal sounds, since artificial sounds can be built up by standard well-known acoustical techniques such as, for example, Fourier synthesis of original sound prototypes. Alternatively, fundamental tones produced by the Synthesizer can be combined in novel ways, not reminiscent of conventional instruments. The output from the Synthesizer is recorded directly on discs rather than on tape. A recording of selected output from this instrument has been released by RCA.[28] On the first side of this record, a step-by-step demonstration of how sounds are built up in the Synthesizer is used to show how a number of musical examples presented on the second side were created. Unfortunately, many of the musical examples presented on this second side of the record are so commonplace and of such minor artistic significance that the potential of this instrument for more artistic purposes has not yet been generally realized. It might also be noted in passing that an elementary discussion of some of the principles of operation of the Synthesizer is printed on the record jacket of this album.

This Synthesizer has been displaced by a second, improved Synthesizer which uses electronic oscillators rather than tuning forks as primary sound sources. It is reported that the effects produced by this newer instrument are decidedly superior to those produced by the earlier model. If this be so, there seems but little question that this instrument represents an important technological step beyond facilities developed in the European studios and that it could be used not only to duplicate all the techniques of these groups, but also to extend considerably beyond their present capacities the study of experimental sound combinations. RCA apparently has no direct interest in this, but they have arranged to let certain composers, specifically, Vladimir Ussachevsky from Columbia University and Milton Babbitt from Princeton University, work with the instrument to evaluate its possibilities for producing experimental music.[29] In this way, it may come about that output from the Synthesizer aesthetically competitive with other experimentation in this general field will be produced. (See also Chapter 7.)

[28] *The Sounds and Music of the RCA Electronic Music Synthesizer,* RCA Victor LM–1922.
[29] M. Babbitt, private communication.

Programmed Music

The generation of music by means of automatic high-speed digital computers is a newer technique than the foregoing types of experimentation and, in fact, to the best of our knowledge, the inception of our experiments with the Illiac marks the first serious study in this field. However, there are historical precedents of a sort which should be considered in order that the experiments be cast into correct perspective. In reviewing these precedents, we emphasize, however, that our own work in no way represents the latest development in a long tradition. There really are no direct precedents, and the material we will now discuss in a way illustrates how little historical background we can cite.

Conventional Program Music. The central body of theory and practice of composition has largely been directly involved with structural principles presumably existing essentially independently of referential nonmusical "meaning." These are the principles of composition of so-called absolute music, music which loosely can be said to exist primarily for its own sake independent of literary or other programmatic connotations. The body of principles so codified is reflected in our practice of writing melodic structures, counterpoint, harmony, instrumentation, and in our use of musical forms (sonata form, variation form, etc.). However, in addition, in the history of Western music, considerable interest has been shown by composers in structural principles superficially more nearly extramusical. One of the most obvious of these, and one which is familiar and generally accepted by most listeners, is the "imitation of nature," a musical tradition with a respectable history, if not always given equal recognition to the so-called higher forms of music. Techniques involving the inclusion of actual extramusical sounds such as cowbells to suggest pastoral scenes by Mahler, the simulation of natural sounds with special devices such as the "wind machine" used by Richard Strauss in his *Alpine Symphony,* the imitation of natural sounds by musical instruments, for example, the simulation of bird calls and storm sounds in Beethoven's *Pastoral Symphony,* the use of horn calls to suggest the hunt in many examples of music, as in Berlioz's *Les Troyens,* for example, all fall into this category. The imitation of visual effects and the use of musical symbols for people and even abstract concepts has also frequently been attempted in program music. Many well-known examples of this, of course, also could be cited. In general, however, it would appear that the more the thing symbolized departs from a purely musical symbol, the more necessary it is that a literal explanation be made available to provide that the intended meaning be properly conveyed to the listener and the more the device employed is regarded with suspicion by musical "purists."

Program music, which is, therefore, music in which referential sound symbols are directly employed or in which a story, a plot of one sort or another, is used to connect the various parts of the composition together, reflects one type of utilization of extramusical concepts by composers. However, having recognized this general domain of compositional activity, let us now consider certain special and unusual types of programmatic music writing.

Eye Music. One persistent form of experimental program music and one which seems at first to be of no musical significance is the technique of writing music to conform to a visual pattern on the written or printed page of musical score. Examples of music of this type from as early as the fifteenth century have survived. Thus, in the period between Machaut and Dufay, particularly at the papal court at Avignon:

. . . musicians . . . began to indulge in complicated rhythmic tricks and in the invention of highly involved methods of notating them. . . . Here we find compositions written in the form of a circle or a heart . . . an indication of the strong hold upon the imagination of the composer that the purely manual business of writing exercised in those days.[30]

In the setting of madrigals, sixteenth-century Italian composers indulged in word painting, not to mention even more overt forms of eye music. *Word painting* denotes the use of minute melismatic melodic word images to illustrate musically individual words in a madrigal. Thus, on the word *mare,* a rolling melody suggesting waves might be employed, while for a descent to the underworld, a descending melody line might be used. *Eye music,* specifically, was an even more extreme departure from conservative practice. This was the use of black and white notes to suggest darkness and light, sadness and joy. Since black and white notes in notation were used then as now to indicate rhythmic differences, it can be seen that the movement or speed of a melody would slow down as the composer changed from black to white notation. The relationship of music as heard to the content of the poem would seem rather tenuous by our conventions. Luca Marenzio

[30] W. Apel, *The Notation of Polyphonic Music, 900–1600,* The Medieval Academy of America, Cambridge, Mass., 1942, as quoted in G. Reese, *Music in the Renaissance,* W. W. Norton & Company, Inc., New York, 1954, p. 11.

(1533–1599) is perhaps the best-known madrigal composer to indulge in word painting and eye music.[31]

This, as might be expected, was a practice roundly condemned by conservative theorists. Zarlino, in particular, denounced the practice in terms of his theory of sensible particulars.[32] However, in spite of the theorists, the writing of eye music has persisted ever since. It was a common practice in the Baroque period, and even Bach, for example, was not adverse to using such devices as ascending melodies to suggest an ascent to Heaven. In more recent times, Charles Ives has experimented with visual program music along with his many other innovations. Thus, in the list of his compositions, as tabulated in the Cowells's recent biography of the composer,[33] we find the following:

Yale-Princeton Game, (August, 1907). The wedge formation piece: notes set on paper like men on the football field—one note runs around left-end for a loss, etc. Includes kazoos. Incomplete; a sketch for a "take-off."

Giants vs. Cubs, (August, 1907). Another sketch for a "take-off," this time a baseball game.

To cite another recent example of eye music, Villa-Lobos has written two pieces, *Melodia da Montanha* (*Serra da Piedade de Bello Horizonte*) and *New York Sky-Line* for piano,[34] composed in the following way:[35]

These are two pieces written according to his [Villa-Lobos'] method of "millimetration" of curves and charts. The outline of a drawing, a photograph, or a chart, is transferred to graph paper, so that the unit of the ordinate corresponds to a chromatic degree, and the unit of the abscissa to a metrical note value. The result is then set down on music paper as a melody. By this method, Villa-Lobos drew the melody of the mountains *Serra da Piedade* at Bello Horizonte. Villa-Lobos has similarly "millimetred" the melody of the sky-line of New York City, and harmonized it. The whole job was done in one hour and

[31] See, for example, A. Einstein, *The Italian Madrigal,* Princeton University Press, Princeton, N.J., vol. I, pp. 234–244.

[32] G. Zarlino, *Istituzioni armoniche,* section 71, as contained in O. Strunk, *Source Readings in Music History,* W. W. Norton & Company, Inc., New York, 1950, pp. 248–251.

[33] H. Cowell and S. Cowell, *Charles Ives and His Music,* Oxford University Press, New York, 1955, p. 219.

[34] H. Villa-Lobos, *Melodia da Montanha* and *New York Sky-Line, New Music Edition,* 16(1):15–17, 1942.

[35] N. Slominsky, "Modern Composers of Brazil," *New Music Edition, loc. cit.,* p. 4.

fifty minutes, between 5 and 6:50 o'clock in the afternoon of February 22, 1940.

One other form of programmed music we might mention in passing is more or less related to the various forms of eye music just considered. This is the use of musical anagrams such as the notes *B, A, C, H* (*H* being the German equivalent of B flat) to symbolize "messages" such as Bach's name in a four-note musical theme. Among well-known composers, Schumann, for example, was particularly addicted to inserting alphabetical references in his music. The *Abegg Variations,* the *Carnaval,* and numerous others of his compositions contain such programmatic devices.[36]

Computational Music. If numerical sequences and patterns are used to establish a musical structure rather than the geometrical appeal of a visual design, we can distinguish yet another variety of programmed music. Outstanding examples survive from as early as the fourteenth and fifteenth centuries again, particularly in the isorhythmic motets of composers such as Machaut and Dunstable, and in the design of mensuration and prolation canons in which each voice is in a different rhythm. A well-known example of this latter technique is the *Prolation Mass* of Ockeghem (ca. 1420–ca. 1495).[37] In modern times, the use of the concept of a tone row made up of all twelve tones of the chromatic scale, as first exploited significantly by Schönberg, is a somewhat similar process, although, with more and more usage, this device is being accepted as a musically "pure" procedure, even though no particularly convincing acoustical justification for its usage seems yet to have been formulated. However, because of its rather intriguing properties of symmetry and its susceptibility to permutation processes such as inversion, retrogression, and so on, the tone row as a musical concept has stimulated experiments in musical form which offer a high degree of arithmetical program content. The works of Schönberg largely contain permutation techniques existing more or less within a context of conventional musical operations and existing in particular reference to pitch successions. This is also basically though somewhat less true of the works of Webern and of contemporary composers such as Milton Babbitt. The latter has investigated permutational techniques derived from relationships inherent in certain highly ordered types of tone-row sequences and has tried to develop compositional techniques which are independent of conventional con-

[36] R. H. Stauffer, *Florestan, the Life and Work of Robert Schumann,* Henry Holt and Company, Inc., New York, 1945, pp. 290–291.

[37] See, for example, Reese, *op. cit.,* pp. 133–136.

siderations of tonality.[38, 39] On the other hand, there has also recently sprung up a different type of serial writing in which not only the tones, but also rhythms, dynamics, and other fundamental musical elements are also controlled, and controlled, it would seem, quite arbitrarily, by means of a "row." Since this "row" now is used to control other elements besides pitch, it exists only as a sequence of numbers which arbitrarily denotes many elements of a composition in addition to pitch. This new type of writing, which has been termed *totally organized music,* is a combination of rhythmic ordering, as apparently first developed by Messiaen,[40, 41] with the twelve-tone concepts of the Schönberg school. In addition to Stockhausen, who has utilized such concepts for the production of *elektronische musik,*[42] Boulez, in particular, has worked out composing schemes of this type.[42-44] Related techniques are exploited by several contemporary Italian composers, such as Nono,[44] Donatoni, Togni, and Maderna.[45] For our purposes, one point in relation to the basic idea of totally organized music itself is worth noting, namely, that the very nature of this concept puts music of this class into an extreme and limited category in terms of modern communication theory. This happens quite independently of its aural effect or of its aesthetic "value." As we pointed out in Chapter 2, both modern aesthetic theory and modern communication theory are based upon an awareness also of the role of lack of organization, of ambiguity or randomness in the structure of messages, including musical ones. This does not exclude the possibility of tonal organization any more than it does the possibility of the total lack of organization, which we consider below. It simply fits it in as one element within the framework of a larger picture. It should

[38] M. Babbitt, "Some Aspects of Twelve-tone Composition," *The Score,* 12:53, 1955; M. Babbitt, *The Function of Set Structure in the Twelve-tone System,* unpublished mimeographed manuscript.

[39] G. Perle, "The Harmonic Problem in Twelve-tone Music," *The Music Review,* 15:257, 1954.

[40] O. Messiaen, *Technique de mon Langage Musicale,* A. Leduc, Paris, 1948.

[41] D. Drew, "Messiaen—A Provisional Study, I." *The Score,* 11:33, 1954; "II," *ibid.,* 13:59, 1955; "III," *ibid.,* 14:41, 1955.

[42] E. Krenek, "New Development in Electronic Music," *Musical America,* 75(11):8, September, 1955. See also articles in vol. 1 of *Die Reihe.*

[43] M. Feldman, P. Boulez, J. Cage, and C. Wolff, Four Musicians at Work," *transformation,* 1:168, 1952.

[44] L. Pestalozza, "Post-Weberniani, concerti ed elettronici," *Ricordiana,* 2:333, 1956; H. Cowell, "Current Chronicle, New York," *The Musical Quarterly,* 38:123, 1952.

[45] R. S. Brindle, "The Lunatic Fringe—III. Computational Composition," *The Musical Times,* 97:354, 1956.

also be noted that the term *totally organized* is also rather misleading, since a totally ordered piece of music would be limited to one pitch, one rhythmic event, one indication of dynamics, and so on.

Mathematical Aesthetics. One other development somewhat related to the above deserves mention. This is the use of mathematical formulations which serve as the underlying groundwork for assembling supposedly aesthetically significant art structures. There have been several fairly substantial attempts in recent years to develop theories of aesthetic value which can be expressed quantitatively by means of algebraic formulas, which in turn can be utilized in arithmetical operations to produce specific "art works." None of these have been employed in our experiments, but it seems desirable to mention at least the more prominent of these theories, since aspects of each might possibly be applied in future experimentation.

The first of these is Birkhoff's theory of aesthetic measure,[46] which he applies to artistic objects in general, although music is singled out for particular consideration. Birkhoff defines a general function called *aesthetic measure, M,* which is the feeling of value which rewards the effort to perceive the *complexity, C,* of an aesthetic object in relation to the realization of its degree of *order, O.* Birkhoff suggests that

$$M = O/C \tag{4}$$

and starting from this premise, he attempts to evaluate the aesthetic measure of forms in geometrical objects, vases, paintings, and, in particular, *conventional* music. Birkhoff devises a number of algebraic formulations which are in excellent accord with conventional harmonic and melodic practice and are suggestive of possible coding techniques for handling this type of music writing. It should be noted, however, that his tendency to associate value with "pleasurable experience" is rather at variance with most contemporary theories of musical aesthetics, such as those we have reviewed in Chapter 2. However, this limitation is not serious, since it affects only the specific forms of the relationships Birkhoff has developed and not the basic method of attack.

A second theory of this general type is the well-known Schillinger system of musical composition,[47] based upon Joseph Schillinger's theory of mathe-

[46] G. D. Birkhoff, *Aesthetic Measure,* Harvard University Press, Cambridge, Mass., 1933.
[47] J. Schillinger, *The Schillinger System of Musical Composition,* Carl Fischer, Inc., New York, 1946.

matical aesthetics.[48] This is a much more ambitious attempt than Birkhoff's to find formulations to characterize aesthetic structures, and, in addition, a reduction to practice, particularly in the field of musical composition, has been worked out. Schillinger goes to some pains to suggest an analogy between his techniques and engineering practice as opposed to supposedly less "scientific" standard musical practices. Since critical analyses of Schillinger's ideas have been published elsewhere,[49] it is perhaps important for us at this time only to note that, to the extent that Schillinger's methods represent a coding of musical techniques into forms convenient for further coding for computer processing, this composing procedure might also be of value in future experimentation with computers.

As one further example, we note the following comments about work by A. H. Frisch, previously referred to,[26] who, by "solving expressions for the squares and cubes of binomials and trinomials, has produced a means of timing for virtually an unlimited number of rhythmic series. . . . Frisch has gone beyond the theoretical work of Schillinger in that he has created the means for mechanically and simply establishing rhythm patterns."

Musical Games and Music by Chance. Hindemith[50] has observed that an English composer named William Hayes in 1751, in a satiric book entitled *The Art of Composing Music by a Method Entirely New, Suited to the Meanest Capacity,* suggested the following compositional technique:

His advice is, to take a brush with stiff bristles (like a toothbrush), dip it into an inkwell, and, by scraping the bristles with the finger, spatter with one sweep a whole composition onto the staff paper. You have only to add stems, bar lines, slurs, et cetera, to make the opus ready for immediate performance. Whole and half notes are entirely absent, but who cares for sustained tones anyway!

This technique, obviously dealt with by Hindemith in uncomplimentary terms, might also be considered an extreme type of eye music. However, if it could be carried out to avoid the building up of any visual design except purely by accident, then pure chance would determine where the notes would fall, in contrast to the other types of eye music previously described. In this music, there would be a lack of any organizing principle, visual or

---

[48] J. Schillinger, *The Mathematical Basis of the Arts,* Philosophical Library, Inc., New York, 1948.

[49] N. Slominsky, *Musical Quarterly,* 32:465, 1946; S. and H. Cowell, *Modern Music,* 23:226, 1946; E. Carter, *ibid.,* 23:228, 1946.

[50] P. Hindemith, *A Composer's World,* Harvard University Press, Cambridge, Mass., 1952, p. 123.

musical, and this music, if correctly prepared, would be a primitive example of what we shall call *random music,* that is, music in which *there is a complete absence of any organizing principle except the laws of probability.*[51] In this random music, moreover, we could predict that all notes would be equally probable. Hale's suggestion, put forward in jest, actually does have some value, since the concept of random music is very useful. As we have already indicated in Chapter 1, the utilization of random-number processes is the basis of our technique for generating computer music. Moreover, the concept also has a definite place in the study of musical aesthetics, as we have pointed out in Chapter 2. It, of course, represents the diametrically opposed musical concept to that of totally organized music just considered.

Obviously the splattering of a manuscript page with ink is an inefficient and untrustworthy method for producing random music, and in recent years other techniques for producing such music have been attempted, notably by John Cage and his followers.[43] Cage has employed tables of random numbers to select musical elements such as notes. Unfortunately, Cage's experiments are burdened with theatrical effects which tend to mask the intrinsic interest of his innovations. Thus, "Cage has often used the I-Ching, an old Chinese method of throwing coins or marked sticks for chance numbers, like our use of dice . . . to ensure that his compositions are 'free of individual taste and memory in their order of events.' He uses a complicated system of charts derived from coin tosses." [52] This was done in the case of the piece being reviewed, namely, *Imaginary Landscape* for twelve radios "played" by twenty-four players plus a conductor. Obviously, the use of the I-Ching today is an absurdly inefficient and pointless way to produce random numbers or, even more so, random-number sequences upon which subsequent restrictions are placed.

Cage has also employed the technique of taking a piece of music for piano written on a number of separate pages and instructing the performer to drop the pages before performance, so that the sequence of the pages and the orientation of each page in the particular performance cannot be predicted. A number of possible "arrangements" of the composition thus become available. Moreover, there are other examples of music by chance written by Cage and composers associated with Cage, such as Morton

---

[51] Strictly speaking, even this music would be organized to the extent that only certain frequencies corresponding to the even-tempered scale would be admitted.

[52] H. Cowell, "Current Chronicle," *Musical Quarterly,* 38:123, 1952.

Feldman, Earl Brown, and Christian Wolff. Thus, Cage himself notes that:[53]

Earl Brown devised a composing procedure in which events following tables of random numbers are written out of sequence, possibly anywhere in a total time row and possibly anywhere else in the same total time text. I myself use chance operations derived from the *I-Ching*, others from the observation of imperfections in the paper upon which I happen to be writing.

The overlap of this last technique with eye music is obvious.

Cage's experiments with dice are by no means a total novelty for there is a limited though definite history of musical games involving chance operations. Of perhaps greatest interest are the musical dice games which were quite a popular novelty in the eighteenth century.[52, 54] Many composers, including J. C. Bach and Mozart, became intrigued with this game. Thus, Mozart is the author of a rather well-known artifact called the *Musikalisches Würfelspiel*. This bore the description[55] "Mozart's musical game, fitted in an elegant box, showing by an easy system to compose an unlimited number of waltzes, rondos, hornpipes and reels—mechanical composition of minuets." This "composition" is at present available in a modern edition.[56]

Some Generalizations. Before we consider experiments involving the generation of music by means of computers, including directly below a review of experiments other than our own, it is perhaps worthwhile to tie together some of the ideas we reviewed in this and the previous chapter.

1. Since modern aesthetic theory and modern communication theory are evolving similar sets of operational concepts, the restatement in musical terms of certain ideas of information theory should yield useful techniques for building up a unified set of critical criteria for evaluating musical experiments. For example, the experiments to produce random music and totally organized music we have just reviewed are really both specific applications of a more generalized procedure involving the control of order-disorder relationships in musical structure.

[53] J. Cage, "Experimental Music," *The Score*, 12:65, 1955.
[54] P. Lowenstein, "Mozart-Kuriosa," *Z. für Musikwissenshaft*, 12:342, 1930; O. E. Deutsch, "Mit Würfeln Komponieren," *ibid.*, 12:595, 1930; H. Gehrigk, "Würfelmusik," *ibid.*, 16:359, 1934.
[55] A. Einstein (ed.), *Köchel's Mozart—Verzeichnis*, 3d ed., J. W. Edwards, Publisher, Inc., Ann Arbor, Mich., 1947, p. 909.
[56] W. A. Mozart, *Musikalisches Würfelspiel*, or *The Dice Composer*, K. anh.294d, (ed. by A. Laszlo), Guild Publications of California, Inc., Hollywood, Calif.

2. Experiments in composing techniques are seen thus far to be distinct in the most part from experiments in producing musical sounds. Some efforts to incorporate logical processes into the production of synthetic music have been noted, but the obviously large area of overlap of techniques has yet to be studied in any detail. This is one area for future research which should prove particularly of interest to experimental composers (see Chapter 7).

3. The process itself for writing music had undergone relatively little change for hundreds of years. Although a number of novel ways for organizing musical information have been devised, aside possibly from certain applications of mathematical formulas, no really significant departures from the traditional techniques of music writing have been developed. This seemed, therefore, the area of research in which coding for computers might really have a profound effect and was the area, therefore, toward which we first directed our attention.

Other Experiments to Generate Computer Music

There seem to be only six other instances thus far, besides our own experiments, of the production of music by means of high-speed electronic digital computers, and in the first case, no actual experimental output has apparently yet been reported. In his recent article discussing certain aspects of information theory and music which we referred to in Chapter 2, R. C. Pinkerton[57] suggested the use of computers for writing simple melodies utilizing an elementary probability table for selecting successive notes of a melody. However, as already indicated, no record of whether this project was actually carried out has been published. Two other projects have both similarly been concerned with the generation of popular or hymn tunes, again by means of probability tables for successive note selection. The first of these experiments was done on the Datatron computer at the ElectroData Division of the Burroughs Corporation in Pasadena, California, by M. Klein and D. Bolitho. This work was publicized in the press,[58] and a reasonably complete semitechnical description of the methods developed by Klein and Bolitho is contained in a company-pub-

---

[57] R. C. Pinkerton, "Information Theory and Melody," *Sci. American,* 194(2):77, February, 1956.

[58] " 'Brain' Computes New Tune for TV," special news release to *The New York Times,* July 3, 1956, p. 16; also Associated Press news release, July 3, 1956.

lished pamphlet.[59] The preparation of a tune called *Push-Button Bertha* for broadcast and recording was carried out. The basic technique utilized was a random-number process combined with successive selection or rejection of these numbers in accord with musical rules translated into arithmetical operations. In principle, therefore, the technique developed by Klein and Bolitho was similar to that utilized by the present authors. It is our understanding, however, that this work has been abandoned.[60]

The second project of a somewhat related nature, since it was also designed to deal with simple tunes, was carried out at Harvard University by Brooks, Hopkins, Neumann, and Wright.[61] The primary purpose of this project was not to generate simple tunes by means of computers but to analyze simple melodies in the light of certain principles of information theory which we shall consider in detail in Chapter 5. It is important to note, however, at this point that a computer was coded by these investigators to produce melodies based upon the laws established by the analytical scheme employed.

Fourthly, according to a recent article in *Computing News*,[62] J. W. Granholm, editor of that magazine, and M. C. Mitchell, oboist at the Seattle Symphony Orchestra, have become interested in possible musical applications of computers. They have carried out preliminary studies of a project to utilize computers for arranging and orchestration. Employing a numbering technique similar to ours for designating the notes of the chromatic scale, they have worked out the problem of transposition for preparing performance parts for transposing instruments. They have also been particularly concerned with the question of musical printout from computers, a problem we shall also consider in Chapter 4.

Fifthly, it has been brought to our attention recently that members of the Shell Laboratories in the Netherlands have used a computer to program Mozart's dice-game composition discussed earlier. However, published information on these experiments was not available at the time of writing. It is our understanding that the coding of this problem was carried out

[59] "Syncopation by Automation," *Data from ElectroData*, August, 1956, Electro-Data Division of Burroughs Corporation, Pasadena, Calif.

[60] Private conversation between one of the present authors (L. A. H.) and Dr. Bolitho in Los Angeles, Aug. 28, 1956.

[61] F. P. Brooks, Jr., A. L. Hopkins, Jr., P. G. Neumann, and W. V. Wright, "An Experiment in Musical Composition," IRE *Trans. on Electronic Computers*, EC-6:175, 1957.

[62] Anon., "Music Transcription by Computer," *Computing News*, 5(17):108–113, Sept. 1, 1957.

by D. A. Caplin, of the Shell Petroleum Company, Ltd., in London.[63]
Lastly, a short piece of computer music has been produced by N. Gutt-man of the Visual and Acoustics Research Department of Bell Telephone Laboratories.[64] This item is of considerable interest in that sounds were synthetically produced on an IBM 704 computer. The composition itself is a short piece in just intonation while the sounds produced by the computer consist of triangular wave forms.

[63] Letter to L. A. H. from Dr. R. J. Lundbeck, Shell Laboratories, the Hague, Netherlands.

[64] Letter to L. A. H. from Dr. J. R. Pierce, Bell Telephone Laboratories, Murray Hill, N.J.

CHAPTER FOUR

The Technical Problem

Non-numerical Uses of Computers

Today, we do not think it unusual that machines can perform arithmetic operations, even rather complex ones; indeed, the current viewpoint is that there is something intrinsically mechanical about such arithmetic operations. On the other hand, it is still considered somewhat unusual whenever the same machines are used to assist other types of thought processes. Non-numerical applications of high-speed computers have been relatively slightly exploited to date, but there now seems to be a rapidly growing interest in the field. For example, at the 11th National Meeting of the Association for Computing Machinery in August, 1956, particular attention was directed toward the new subject of non-numerical uses of high-speed digital computers and served to focus attention on the subject. A review of applications of this type was presented through papers on the following topics: weather prediction,[1] logistics applications,[2] programming

[1] P. D. Thompson, "High-Speed Computing in Weather Prediction," Program and Abstracts for the 11th National Meeting of the Association for Computing Machinery at the University of California at Los Angeles, Aug. 27–29, 1956, p. 6.

[2] W. H. Marlow, "Some Logistics Applications," *ibid.*, p. 6, p. 12.

computers to play games such as chess and checkers,[3] language translation[4] and language compiling.[5] At the same meeting, as noted already in Chapter 1, a brief report of the present work was also given. In more recent meetings, a trend toward the presentation of such topics has been continued.[6]

It is convenient, perhaps, to classify present uses of computers into three broad categories. The first is the obvious category of solving complex mathematical problems in the sciences and engineering, in mathematics, and in other fields in which specific quantitative information is required. These direct mathematical applications are self-evident uses for computers and require no particular comment.

Somewhat less obvious in terms of the basic information supplied the computers is the second category of applications, namely, to business and industrial procedures. Here the applications include, for example, the processing of office data, the simulation and design of industrial-plant operations, and the control of industrial operations through digital-computer control of specialized analog computers and servo-mechanisms. Indeed, these applications are now beginning to attract widespread attention and account for a large proportion of the sales of commercial high-speed automatic digital computers. From the rapidly growing literature on this subject, we can cite representative surveys.[7] A condensed source of current information on these topics is contained in the abstracts in the IRE *Transactions on Electronic Computers*. An introductory review of this subject recently published in *Fortune* might also be cited.[8] Goodman's book,[7]

[3] A. L. Samuel, "Programming a Computer to Play Games," *ibid.*, p. 8, p. 21; see also J. Kister, P. Stein, S. Ulan, W. Walden, and M. Wells, "Experiments in Chess," *J. Assoc. Computing Machinery*, 4:174, 1957.

[4] I. Wieselman, "The Potentialities of a High-capacity Store for Machine Translation," *ibid.*, p. 8, p. 22; also typewritten copy of presentation through courtesy of author.

[5] J. Chipps, M. Koschmann, A. Perlis, S. Orgel, and J. Smith, "A Mathematical Language Compiler," *ibid.*, p. 9, p. 27.

[6] For example, in the program of the 1957 Eastern Joint Computer Conference, Washington, D.C., Dec. 9–13, 1957, the following titles are noted: I. Rotkin, "Mechanization of Letter-mail Sorting"; D. L. Gerlough, "Control of Automobile Traffic as a Problem in Real-time Computation"; W. H. Thomas, "The Application of Electronic Computers to Air Traffic Control."

[7] L. L. Goodman, *Man and Automation,* Penguin Books, Inc., Baltimore, 1957; Scientific American, *Automatic Control,* Simon and Schuster, Inc., New York, 1955; E. M. Grabbe (ed.), *Automation in Business and Industry,* John Wiley & Sons, Inc., New York, 1955; J. Diebold, *Automation,* D. van Nostrand Company, Inc., Princeton, N.J., 1952.

[8] W. B. Harris, "The Astonishing Computers," *Fortune,* 55(6):136, June, 1957.

which is a useful treatment of the subjects of automation and computers written in nontechnical language, includes detailed descriptions of actual examples of computers now in operation in the business world. Goodman points out that this type of application is basically of a non-numerical nature when he notes that:[9]

In business use, it is the ability of the computer to organize and sort data which is more important than its ability to do arithmetic; though . . . the ability to solve complex mathematical problems is necessary when decision-making of a managerial nature is undertaken. The office is now quickly becoming a "factory" for the processing of data and it is in this light that electronic data processing should be viewed.

The final category includes other types of non-numerical applications and covers, of course, a wide range of possible fields of interest.[10] In addition to some of the more important applications already mentioned, it is interesting to note that even in the sciences auxiliary applications of a non-numerical type are being developed. In the field of medicine, for example, it is predicted that computers will be used in conjunction with medical diagnosis, since these instruments will not only be able to store known medical information and patients' case histories, but they will also be able to sift this information to assist the actual process of diagnosis.[11] In the field of chemistry, one application is the storing of formulas for chemical compounds;[12] another is their use to speed up patent searches in

[9] Goodman, op. cit., p. 56.

[10] The following item, which we noted in the Sept. 21, 1957, issue of The New Yorker, gives one indication of the extent of these applications: "Systematic permutations of the Tibetan alphabet with an automatic sequence computer aided lamas high in the Himalaya mountains in discovering all the possible names for God, approximately nine billion of them. Why they undertook this problem is a matter for metaphysical speculation. At work on the project for three centuries, the lamas figured it would require another 15 thousand years to complete the project by hand. However, with a Mark V computer the task was accomplished in 100 days.

"Technicians who accompanied the computer to Tibet report the job was successfully completed. Miles of paper covered with what appeared to be gibberish were turned out by the computer and patiently pasted in huge ledgers by the lamas. The chief lama, in a philosophical dissertation given to the technicians, said that God's purpose has now been achieved and the human race has finished the job it was created to perform. What happens next?

—Automatic Control."

[11] Anon., "Sarnoff Foresees Voice-controlled Systems," Research and Engineering, 3(7):23, October, 1957.

[12] A. Opler and T. R. Norton, "New Speed to Structural Searches," Chem. Eng. News, 34:2812, 1956.

the U.S. Patent Office;[13] and it has even been reported that a computer has been used to compile a list of 42,000 names with endings like -*mycin* to be given to future antibiotics and drugs.[14]

Of the various applications cited, perhaps the use of computers for translating foreign languages can be singled out as the one most related to our problem. A historical survey of this problem has been written by W. N. Locke.[15] This, at the present time, is a high-priority research project, financed primarily by the United States government, because there are far too few translators available for the translation of contemporary Russian technical literature into English. Technical literature, with its relatively restricted vocabulary and relatively small use of shades of meaning, idioms, and similar more difficult translation problems, turns out to be a most suitable test medium for this type of study. It should not be supposed, however, that all interest in this field is confined to the limited and specific objective of translating technical Russian. The broader objectives of being able to interconvert all languages and to handle nontechnical literature are also being examined. For this purpose, an "interlingua" for machine usage is also being examined. Each language is first translated into interlingua and then converted into the "target" language. Interest in the general subject of machine translation is now sufficiently great that a monograph[16] has been written on the subject and a periodical, *Mechanical Translation,* devoted exclusively to this subject, now exists. There are already available rather impressive examples of the results of machine translation, even at this early date. The goal for the present appears to be total conversion to the words of the target language, i.e., English, in the specific applications discussed above, with about ninety per cent accuracy on grammar and other problems such as multiple meanings. Texts in this condition can be rapidly edited into literate English.

In light of these experiments, the generation of musical structures is a rather natural non-numerical application of these instruments, since, like mathematical or alphabetical symbols, musical symbols can be operated upon in a wide variety of ways to produce a virtually limitless number of combinatorial forms.

[13] Anon., "Electronic Searching Moves Ahead," *Chem. Eng. News,* 35:98, 1957; also *Patent Office, Research and Development, Reports 4–9.*

[14] Anon., "Drugless Names," *Chem. Eng. News,* 34:774, 1956.

[15] W. N. Locke, "Translation by Machine," *Sci. American,* 194(1):29, January, 1956.

[16] W. N. Locke and A. D. Booth (eds.), *Machine Translation of Languages,* John Wiley & Sons, Inc., New York, 1955.

Operation of Automatic High-speed Digital Computers

Before we consider the experimental methods used to produce music by means of the Illiac, it is desirable to describe briefly in general terms the basic operations of automatic high-speed electronic digital computers. Goodman[7] describes their operations somewhat more completely, and detailed discussions of their construction and operation are available in the literature.[17]

Automatic high-speed digital computers are devices capable of performing the arithmetic operations of addition, subtraction, multiplication, and division in time intervals of the order of milliseconds. If these instruments were nothing more than high-speed desk calculators, we would be unable to take advantage of the increased speed of computation since human reaction times are much slower than computer reaction times. This is to be contrasted with the use of ordinary desk calculators, where machine and human reaction times are "well balanced." Consequently, in order to be efficient, high-speed computers require instructions supplied at rates of the order of magnitude of the rates of their arithmetic operations. This requirement has led to the "automation" of high-speed computing. In the automatic high-speed digital computer, a list of instructions is placed into the machine and automatically selected in sequence at speeds commensurate with the arithmetic operations. The preparation of the list of instructions for the computer is referred to as *coding,* or *programming,* and the total collection of instructions to which the machine can respond is called the *code* or *program.* Problems to be solved by the computer must be reduced to a pattern of instructions which are repeated over and over again, and normally only the numbers being operated on undergo significant change. These patterns of instructions are called *loops,* or *cycles.*

Since most problems require decisions to be made, the list of instructions for the computer must include, besides arithmetic orders, an order for making decisions. Of course, the coder must foresee the decisions to be made and plan for them accordingly. The most usual type of decision order is one in which there are two possible results, e.g., plus or minus, zero or non-

---

[17] See, for example, E. C. Berkeley and L. Wainwright, *Computers, Their Operation and Application,* Reinhold Publishing Corporation, New York, 1956; T. E. Ivall (ed.), *Electronic Computers, Principles and Applications,* Philosophical Library, Inc., New York, 1956; G. R. Stibitz and J. A. Larrivee, *Mathematics and Computers,* McGraw-Hill Book Company, Inc., New York, 1957.

zero. When this decision order appears in the sequence of instructions, it either leaves the sequencing unchanged, as if it were not there at all, or it transfers, or "jumps," the sequencing to another part of the list of instructions. A common name for this type of decision order is *conditional transfer order*.

To hold the instructions or numbers, a computer requires a storage unit, sometimes called the *memory,* and a programmer must have available corresponding orders to store and obtain information from this unit within the machine.[18] There must also be communication between the computer and the outside, necessitating an input and output mechanism and corresponding orders. In the case of the Illiac, input and output are prepared in the form of Teletype tape. Input is prepared in the form of coded punched tape on Teletype machines, while output can be transcribed back into printed numbers or letters by means of electronic-tape readers attached to these same Teletype machines. With other instruments, input and output is often prepared in the form of punched cards or magnetic tape.

Some of the more important units and orders for a computer are summarized in Table 1. The details of coding for the Illiac in particular are

Table 1
Important Units and Orders for a Computer

Unit	*Order*
Arithmetic	Add, subtract, multiply, divide
Storage	Store, read from storage
Input	Read
Output	Punch, print, cathode ray tube display, etc.
Decision	Conditional transfer
Miscellaneous	Unconditional transfer, left shift, right shift, shift registers, etc.

discussed in a programming guide prepared for use with this machine.[19]

Computers like the Illiac perform arithmetic in much the same way we do with pencil and paper except that they use the binary number system rather than the more common everyday decimal number system. This number system is particularly appropriate, because circuits in the computer either conduct or do not conduct; that is to say, these circuits operate through vacuum tubes used as electronic relays. These exist in either of

[18] L. N. Ridenour, "Computer Memories," *Sci. American,* 192(6):92, June, 1955.
[19] J. P. Nash (ed.), *Illiac Programming,* Digital Computer Laboratory, Graduate College. University of Illinois, Urbana, Ill., 1955, and later printings. A more general discussion of computer programming is contained in D. D. McCracken, *Digital Computer Programming,* John Wiley & Sons, Inc., New York, 1957.

two states, conducting or nonconducting. To understand the binary number system, let us first examine the more familiar decimal notation, consisting of ten symbols, 0, 1, 2, . . . , 9, with which we can write any number. For example, in the decimal number 121.51, three 1s appear, each representing a different absolute magnitude depending on its position with respect to the decimal point.

We can also rewrite the above number in the following way:

$$121.51 = 1 \times 10^2 + 2 \times 10^1 + 1 \times 10^0 + 5 \times 10^{-1} + 1 \times 10^{-2} \quad (5)$$

And, in general, we can write any decimal number as

$$b_n 10^n + b_{n-1} 10^{n-1} + \cdots + b_1 10^1 + b_0 10^0 + b_{-1} 10^{-1} + \cdots + b_{-m} 10^{-m} \quad (6)$$

where $0 \leq b_j \leq 9$. However, there is nothing unique about the number ten as a base for a number system. Let us consider two as a base for a number system with only the symbols 0, 1. If we impose the restriction that $a_i = 0, 1$, we can write numbers as

$$a_n 2^n + a_{n-1} 2^{n-1} + \cdots + a_1 2^1 + a_0 2^0 + a_{-1} 2^{-1} + \cdots + a_{-m} 2^{-m} \quad (7)$$

For example, the decimal number 10 (ten) can be written in the binary number system as 1010 which is

$$1 \times 2^3 + 0 \times 2^2 + 1 \times 2^1 + 0 \times 2^0 = 8 + 0 + 2 + 0 = 10 \quad (8)$$

In Table 2, we have tabulated the correspondence between decimal and binary notation for the first sixteen integers.

Table 2
Decimal and Binary Integers

Decimal number	Binary number
0	0
1	1
2	10
3	11
4	100
5	101
6	110
7	111
8	1000
9	1001
10	1010
11	1011
12	1100
13	1101
14	1110
15	1111

It is this technical detail involving binary numbers of computer design that lies behind Shannon and Weaver's comment:[20] "The choice of a logarithmic base corresponds to the choice of a unit for measuring information. If the base 2 is used the resulting units may be called *binary digits*, or more briefly, *bits*, a word suggested by J. W. Tukey."

The "Man-versus-Machine" Problem

One subject which must be considered at this point is whether the new-type computers "think." Outside the computer field, there exist many misconceptions concerning what computers can and cannot do. Thus, almost inevitably, when the subject of our work has come up, the question has been asked: "What is going to happen to the composer?", the implication being that the composer is going to be put out of business by an "electronic brain."

Much of what is said about computers depends on how one defines the word *think*. A commonly accepted picture of a computer is that of a machine which is an extension in certain specific functions of human intelligence, much as a physical machine such as a steam engine is an extension of human physical strength, also in certain specified directions. As we have seen, a digital computer, or for that matter an analog computer, is capable of doing certain mathematical tasks more rapidly and more efficiently than a human being can. These computers respond to detailed instructions as to what calculations to perform, carry out these instructions, and present the results to the operator, who then has to determine whether these results are useful or meaningful depending upon the nature of the problem being solved. The computer is unable to determine whether the answers are correct. It can perform erroneous calculations just as efficiently as correct ones. This is why some writers have spoken of a computer programmer "conversing" with a computer. He feeds it certain information and tells the computer what to do with the information. The computer carries out the instructions, and then the programmer inspects the results.

Aids to calculation are hardly a new departure in human affairs. The abacus, published tables of mathematical functions, the slide rule, the common adding machine, and the desk calculator are all precursors of the present highly developed computers. All of these aids to calculation can be considered to displace the operation of human intelligence to lesser or greater

[20] C. E. Shannon and W. Weaver, *The Mathematical Theory of Communication*, University of Illinois Press, Urbana, Ill., 1949, p. 4.

extent in certain specific functions. For example, long division carried out on paper requires mental effort over a significant period of time, whereas the same operation can be mechanized and solved with the aid of a desk calculator in a few seconds. To the extent that this specific mental effort is called "thinking," even an ordinary desk calculator can be said to "think." However, with most fairly simple machines such as desk calculators, the human functions displaced by the machine have hardly been regretted. However, writers such as Goodman are careful to distinguish between mechanization and automation and to point out that the effect of automation upon man should be quite the opposite to that of mechanization. Goodman notes that:[21]

Charles Chaplin's *Modern Times* (made in 1935), by exposing the fallacy in Henry Ford's doctrine of the "one man, one operation" concept, exemplifies all that automation will eliminate. Such boring, repetitive, soul-breaking work will not be required to be done in the future by human beings—a human being possesses judgement, imagination, flexibility, and great powers of coordination . . . whereas the machine may be better from the point of view of strength and perception, man is irreplaceable.

With a digital computer, automation, made possible through such operations as the conditional transfer order previously described, eliminates this "single-operation-plus-inspection" process required in the use of desk calculators. Rapid routine calculations become possible. However, the total course of a calculation must be foreseen by the operator, even though the specific results cannot be predicted, and the method for solving the mathematical problem must be worked out, even though the form of the answer is unknown. Similarly, in a musical problem, the method of composition must be coded, even though the final *specific* outcome may be unpredictable.

There are research efforts continually going on to improve the performance of computing machines. By simply making their internal works more complex and by increasing their storage capacity, more complicated problems can be handled. The increased bulk of instruments of larger capacity can be compensated to some extent by replacement of vacuum tubes by transistors and magnetic core devices. Other more basic changes include improved input and output mechanisms and high-capacity storage or memory. The advance in usefulness of computers will, therefore, rest partially on technological improvements and the building of more complex and ver-

---

[21] Goodman, *op. cit.*, p. 21.

satile instruments. On the other hand, more complex logical operations to which these computers might be adapted must also be anticipated. In fact, a problem receiving considerable attention today is the analysis of the problems of "adaptability" and "learning." The question of whether these processes can be coded to activate computers to respond in these terms has been considered.[22] In fact, the general study of comparing men and machines, for which Wiener[23] coined the word *cybernetics,* is based upon analyzing the various response mechanisms of man in terms of the concepts of automation. This includes such principles as "closed-loop control" which are basic to automation theory. Another similarity is recognized through the concept of "purposeful action" which suggests that present activity is motivated in terms of future goals and which, we might also note, bears a striking similarity to some of Meyer's concepts, considered in Chapter 2, of directed musical motion. It is not difficult to formulate comparisons of computer circuits and the nervous system and to attempt, by finding mechanical and electrical analogs to the nervous system, to analyze by these analogies the logical foundation of the actual thought process. In fact, some writers suggest that the essential difference between the best computers and man is really just one of complexity. Kermeny[24] proposes that the two basic things which differentiate man and computers are complexity of memory and power of reproduction. The other factors, suitable input devices (i.e., sense organs) and output devices (i.e., equivalents to human actions) are being developed, presumably along with sufficiently complex programming techniques to instill learning capacity. Other writers take a much less daring view and suggest that the problem of building a machine of the complexity of memory equivalent to man's is not really feasible, at least in terms of techniques we can consider today or in the near future. Moreover, they suggest also that the qualities of human actions are far from being understood in terms of coding. Since these are questions which can only be decided in the future, we may conclude that, for the present, computers are still definitely limited to specific tasks in which one type or another of data processing are of a fairly routine nature.

The question of whether computers will ever be "creative" in the sense that we speak of creative composing is rather similar to the problem of

[22] A. G. Oettinger, "Programming a Digital Computer to Learn," *Phil. Mag.,* 7:1243, 1952; C. E. Shannon, "Computers and Automation," *Proc.* I.R.E., 41:1234, 1953.
[23] N. Wiener, *Cybernetics,* John Wiley & Sons, Inc., New York, 1949, in particular, Introduction and chap. 5.
[24] J. G. Kermeny, "Man Viewed as a Machine," *Sci. American,* 192(4):58, April, 1955.

whether they "think." Also, we might ask: "What is meant by the term creative?" Being "creative" would seem to depend at the very minimum, like "thinking," on having a computer operate on a self-sustaining basis, and to "learn from experience." If we postulate, therefore, that creative actions involve, at the very least, a unique perception of relationships between apparently disassociated events in such a way that a new truth is disclosed, then creativity seems to be bound up with the question of ignorance. Moreover, it seems that what we first consider strokes of insight and manifestations of "creative thought" are, once they are analyzed and codified and, particularly, codified to the extent that they can be processed by a computer, no longer "creative processes" in the usual sense. Seen in this light, the pursuit of knowledge which depends on "creative thought" is a technique of coding, of finding explicit statements of more and more complex logical relationships. If "creativity" is defined in such terms, then the question of whether machines can do this type of coding is the one which has to be answered. The present computers, even though they may be programmed to process problems in music, for example, cannot be expected to seek out new musical principles. These now must be fed to the machine in explicit detail, and, at best, the uncertainty introduced by freedom of choice, i.e., the use of the random-number processes which we have applied to produce computer music, perhaps gives a computer a very primitive sort of unpredictability, but this can hardly be equated to any sort of creative process.

The Monte Carlo Method

The practical technical method employed for generating computer music is based on the so-called "Monte Carlo method," which we shall describe first in general terms[25] and secondly in terms of its specific application to musical problems.

The Monte Carlo method is a rather new experimental technique based, as the name is meant to suggest, upon the operation of the laws of chance. In essence, the method is quite simple, involving basically an examination

[25] D. D. McCracken, "The Monte Carlo Method," *Sci. American,* 192(5):90, May, 1955; G. R. Stibitz and J. A. Larrivee, *op. cit.,* chap. 9; A. S. Householder (ed.), *Monte Carlo Method,* Applied Mathematics Series, no. 12, National Bureau of Standards, U.S. Government Printing Office, 1951. These references, and the first two in particular, are general introductions to the idea of the Monte Carlo method. There are, of course, many specialized technical articles in the literature on the method and its application.

of sets of randomly selected numbers which we consider to represent significant sets of events in some model universe. The method is justified in instances where the object of study can be assumed to be a statistically ordered universe from which we can isolate certain elements to form a simpler model universe characterized by events subject to the same statistical order. Thus, the Monte Carlo method consists of the experimental production of random sets which are made to conform to statistical controls. It permits us, therefore, to study the laws presumably implicit in the statistical controls chosen for the experiment. Since experimental results are obtained in random sequence by this method, it is distinguished from more traditional laboratory experimentation in which significant environmental factors are systematically varied or controlled. An additional assumption is often made that many events are normally made up of smaller events and that if these smaller events can be caused to occur in the proper manner, for example, as sequential patterns, combinations of these events can be generated which will include the classes of larger events of interest. The Monte Carlo method gives us a sampling from the model universe, and this sampling may then be compared to presumably analogous or at least similar events in the natural universe. Normally, such a comparison is made to develop an hypothesis concerning the events of the real world or else to refine the model so that it conforms more exactly in the next experiment to the aspects of the real universe being examined.

There is one major penalty attached to the Monte Carlo method in its purest form. In almost any given experiment, many superfluous events occur which are of no interest unless the process under examination happens to be truly and completely random. In a practical experiment, this means that a screening procedure must be devised to eliminate the superfluous events in the most efficient manner. Until recently, the inefficiency of the Monte Carlo method limited its application to relatively simple problems. In principle, it is possible to run a Monte Carlo experiment by hand methods, for example, by compiling a random-number table by some simple arithmetical process, categorizing these numbers according to the demands of the problem under investigation, and, in due time, completing the experiment. Unfortunately, hand methods are too slow for any but the simplest sort of problems, problems for which more conventional analytical methods are much more satisfactory. With the development of high-speed computers, however, this situation has been radically changed, for these instruments are able to examine and process many millions of numbers per hour. Thus, the Monte Carlo method is finally coming into its own, since it can now be applied to many complex problems of a statistical nature which have so far resisted solution by analytical means.

A second basic feature of the Monte Carlo method involves the nature of the procedure required for sampling. In other words, how do we go about collecting a set of samples from our model universe? It is seen that the only practical method for carrying out the sampling procedure itself is the sequential one—that is, one sample at a time is analyzed for the properties of interest and is then placed into its proper category. Practical everyday sampling procedures, such as public opinion surveys, industrial quality-control techniques, and so on, can all be resolved in principle to this idea of a step-by-step process. The important next step, then, is to build up a theory to analyze both the distribution of samples and how this distribution is affected by the particular restrictions placed upon the rules governing the sampling process itself. To do this, use is made of the theory of probability and of classical problems of chance, such as the drawing of colored balls from an urn. It is not necessary to go into details, but it is essential to present at least an illustration of such an operation so that we may define several terms useful in the analysis of *sequential*, or *chain*, *processes*, as they are also often called.

Let us consider an urn containing five white, three black, and two red balls. If we let the basic event be the drawing of a ball of a definite color, it is possible to designate the three possible events as E_w, a white ball, E_b, a black ball, and E_r, a red ball. We may now construct a mathematical model in which the events are represented by points. The collection of all such points is called the event space s. There is a law of probability called the *probability distribution function*, or simply the *distribution function*, which defines the probability p, for each point of our event space s. For example, $p(E_w) = 5/(5 + 3 + 2) = \frac{1}{2}$. However, instead of trying to describe a function over the points of s, it is often simpler to associate the points of s with numbers and describe a distribution function over these numbers. The function that associates numbers with the points of s is called a *stochastic variable*, or *random variable*, or *chance variable*. We can, for example, define the following stochastic variable x for the balls in the urn:

	E_w	E_b	E_r	
x	0	1	2	(9)

The function that describes the probability of x is called the *probability function* $f(x)$. Thus, for balls in the urn:

$$f(0) = 0.5$$
$$f(1) = 0.3 \qquad (10)$$
$$f(2) = 0.2$$

Let us now consider a sequence of drawings from the urn under the following conditions:

1. After each drawing the ball will be replaced.
2. If the color of the ball is the same as that of the preceding drawing, the ball will be returned to the urn without the event being recorded.

A process which depends on the preceding event only is an example of a simple *Markoff process,* and the corresponding sequence is called a *Markoff chain.* Now, if we let $\mathrm{pr}(E)$ be the probability of the event E and let $\mathrm{pr}_{E_1}(E)$ be the probability of the event E, given the previous event was E_1, for the above sequence, we have the following probabilities:

1. Initially:

$$\mathrm{pr}(E_w) = 0.5, \qquad \mathrm{pr}(E_b) = 0.3, \qquad \mathrm{pr}(E_r) = 0.2 \qquad (11)$$

2. Succeeding probabilities:

$$\mathrm{pr}_{E_w}\,(E_w) = 0, \qquad \mathrm{pr}_{E_w}\,(E_b) = 3/5, \qquad \mathrm{pr}_{E_w}\,(E_r) = 2/5$$
$$\mathrm{pr}_{E_b}\,(E_w) = 5/7, \qquad \mathrm{pr}_{E_b}\,(E_b) = 0, \qquad \mathrm{pr}_{E_b}\,(E_r) = 2/7 \qquad (12)$$
$$\mathrm{pr}_{E_r}\,(E_w) = 5/8, \qquad \mathrm{pr}_{E_r}\,(E_b) = 3/8, \qquad \mathrm{pr}_{E_r}\,(E_r) = 0$$

The concept of chain processes is thus a useful analytical tool for processing experimental data obtained by the Monte Carlo method. Moreover, in terms of information theory, chain processes are also seen to have broader implications in that the quantitative description of discrete-channel communication systems depends upon the analysis of how discrete symbols are chosen sequentially. It is in view of this fact that Shannon and Weaver define their terms relevant to sequential operations and make use of the concepts of stochastic variable and of Markoff processes already introduced. These authors give a particularly simple definition of a stochastic process as follows:[26]

We can think of a discrete source as generating the message, symbol by symbol. It will choose successive symbols according to certain probabilities depending, in general, on preceding choices as well as the particular symbols in question. A physical system, or a mathematical model of a system which produces such a sequence of symbols governed by a set of probabilities, is known as a stochastic process.

[26] Shannon and Weaver, *op. cit.,* p. 10.

Shannon and Weaver also define Markoff processes and distinguish between zeroth-order processes in which transition probabilities are independent of previous events, being fixed a priori; first-order processes in which there is a dependence of the probabilities upon only the immediately preceding event, as in the above example involving balls being drawn from an urn; and higher-order processes in which more than just the immediately preceding event is involved.

It is now necessary to make note of at least one or two applications of the Monte Carlo method somewhat more elegant than the drawing of colored balls from an urn. This is important because the significance of the method is obscured if we consider only simple physical situations for which analytical solutions are readily obtained, as in the above case. A somewhat more complex application, for example, might be the analysis of the diffusion of gas molecules or of particles suspended in a liquid to derive Fick's laws of diffusion. Since diffusion depends upon the random motions of molecules, the method of *random flights* may be used to simulate this process. A random flight is defined as the particular species of Markoff chain in which equally weighted a priori transition probabilities are assigned to all possible choices for each successive event, i.e., each possible choice is equally probable. This is again a situation we have encountered previously in the discussion of information theory and is the situation characterized in information theory as having the maximum entropy content.

The random-flight technique can also be applied to other problems. If restrictions are placed upon the randomness of choice either by weighting the transition probabilities unequally or by forbidding certain choices, other situations in nature, of lower entropy content, may also be simulated. For example, by forbidding the return of a random flight to a point in space previously occupied, it is possible to generate elementary models for flexible long-chain polymer molecules such as rubber and other plastic materials. This last problem was worked on by the present authors in connection with another research project.[27] The Illiac was used also for this work, and, in fact, this earlier study is mentioned here because some of the

[27] F. T. Wall, L. A. Hiller, Jr., and D. J. Wheeler, "Statistical Computation of Mean Dimensions of Macromolecules—I," *J. Chem. Phys.*, 22:1036, 1954; F. T. Wall, L. A. Hiller, Jr., and W. F. Atchison, "Statistical Computation of Mean Dimensions of Macromolecules—II," *ibid.*, 23:913, 1955; "III," *ibid.*, 23:2314, 1955; "IV," *ibid.*, 26:1742, 1957; F. T. Wall, R. J. Rubin, and L. M. Isaacson, "Improved Statistical Method for Computing Mean Dimensions of Macromolecules," *ibid.*, 27:186, 1957.

programming employed for that problem was used to initiate the work in musical composition to be discussed. The connection seems less far-fetched once we recall that the process of composition can be conceived as a complex random flight through a tonal universe, with dimensions of pitch and time subject to restrictions we normally associate with rules of composition.

The Monte Carlo Method and the Generation of Music

Since the Monte Carlo method generates as well as processes data, it is the obvious technique for producing musical notes, rhythms, and other musical elements. As a first experiment, we decided to assign integer values to the white notes of the musical scale and generate integers at random which could be processed in turn in such a way as to build up machine representations of extremely simple musical structures. The technical problem for this initial experiment was separated into four basic parts. The first was the relatively simple problem of generating random sequences of integers which, in this early experiment, were equated to the white notes from C below middle C to C above middle C. For this scale, therefore, a range of values 0 through 14 were used since fifteen notes were involved. As long as random sequences of these integers were not processed in any way and were simply printed out as produced, we generated random white-note music. This, as our previous discussion would indicate, is a universe of all white-note music, both "good" and "bad." The question then arose of how to distinguish samples which are "good" from those which are not. To do this, we processed the randomly generated notes through a *sorting process*, or *sieve*, accepting some notes and rejecting others. This sorting process was the second and by far the most complex part of the problem of generating computer music. Thirdly, the accepted notes had to be stored in the memory of the computer and assembled step by step into a machine representation of a finished musical "composition." Lastly, this "composition," in turn, was converted into a printed representation in number or letter notation, which was then transcribed by hand into musical score.

Propagation of Random Sequences of Integers. An uninstructed computer obviously produces nothing by itself. Therefore, even the generation of random sequences of integers must be provided for in a set of input instructions. Since a computer can only operate in an orderly fashion, i.e., "according to rules," it cannot "run wild" and produce random integers by accident. Hence, we had to devise an *orderly* method of producing random integers. There are a number of procedures for propagating sequences of random or, at least, pseudo-random integers.[28] The one we have chosen is the following. Let us express a fraction f, represented in the number system base a, in the number system base b, i.e., let us find the c_i such that:

$$f = c_1 b^{-1} + c_2 b^{-2} + \cdots + c_n b^{-n} + \cdots \qquad (13)$$

where $0 \leqq c_i \leqq b - 1$. If we multiply Equation (13) by b, we have:

$$bf = c_1 + c_2 b^{-1} + \cdots + c_n b^{-n+1} + \cdots \qquad (14)$$

The integer part of bf is equal to c_1. After subtracting c_1 from Equation (14), we may repeat this operation by another multiplication and in this way generate the digits of yet a new representation. If f cannot be represented exactly in the new base, the process will not terminate, i.e., the residual fraction will never be zero. If the digits of f are reasonably random initially, the digits of the new representation will also be random. To generate random integers in a binary machine, we can take the digits of a transcendental, for example, such as 0.1π, or any other convenient irrational number, and use the process of Equation (14) where b equals the range of random integers desired. If b is a multiple of 2, to prevent the process of Equation (14) from terminating, the base $b + 1$ is used, and one random integer, say b, is always rejected. This process was examined rather carefully in a previous research project[27] and appears to give integers in random sequence which showed no evidence of recycling after 840,000 trials.

As a concrete illustration of how this process operates, the hand computation of a random sequence of seven digits, 0, 1, 2, 3, 4, 5, and 6, is shown in Table 3. In this example, we start with a four-digit decimal fraction $f = 0.2718$ and with $b = 7$. The random sequence of integers, as shown in Table 3, is 1, 6, 2, 1, 4, ...

This example demonstrates that this random integer generation process accomplishes two important things. (1) It provides a mechanism for obtaining a sequence of random digits. (2) It also serves to keep the random digits in the range of a selected number system defined by the parameter b.

Statistical Tests and the "Try-again" Method. The first experiment attempted was the writing of simple melodies, using only the following four rules for successive melodic intervals: (1) no tritones are permitted; (2)

[28] See, for example, Stibitz and Larrivee, *op. cit.*, pp. 188–191.

Table 3
The Generation of Random Integers

0.2718
× 7
———————
1. / .9026
× 7
———————
6. / .3182
× 7
———————
2. / .2274
× 7
———————
1. / .5918
× 7
———————
4. / .1426
.

.

.

Random-integer sequence:
1, 6, 2, 1, 4, . . .

no sevenths are permitted; (3) the melody must start and end on middle C; and (4) the range of the melody from its highest to lowest note must not exceed one octave. This we shall term the *octave-range rule*. Melodies varying in length from three to twelve notes were generated, the notes being chosen at random. Whenever a rule was violated, the melody attempt was terminated and the whole process was started over again. The rules were sufficiently few in number so that it was expected that a reasonable fraction of the attempted melodies would be completed successfully. The statistics of this melody-generation process are shown in Figure 1, where the ratio of successful to total (successful plus unsuccessful) melodic attempts is plotted against the length of the melody. It is seen that the longer the melody is required to be, the less chance there is of completing the melody, since the probability of violating some one of the rules increases as the length of the melody is increased. Since these statistics depend on several arbitrarily chosen rules of composition, no attempt was made to find significant correlations. It was noted, however, that with the addition of more rules, the probability of obtaining a successful piece of music would soon become very small, so in order to generate music more efficiently, a *try-again method* was introduced instead. In this method, instead of rejecting the whole of a partially completed "composition" upon the violation of a rule, only the note which violates the rule is rejected and another note is generated to replace it. This process is permitted to continue until a successful note is obtained or until it becomes apparent that

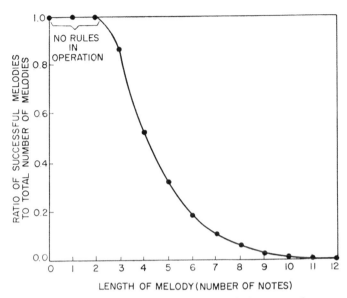

LENGTH OF MELODY (NUMBER OF NOTES)

Figure 1. Statistics of elementary melody generation.

no such note exists, in which case, the "composition" is erased and a new "composition" started. In the experiments to be discussed, the number of trials was set at fifty by a simple counting index of the type described in detail under Experiment Two in Chapter 5.

Four points should be emphasized in regard to the try-again method: (1) We do not have to normalize for any unequal weighting given the various possible melodies generated by means of any particular set of composition rules. This is in contrast to many experiments describing physical situations in which the statistics must be adjusted in accord with the principle of equipartition of energy. In our case, it is sufficient only that, in the generation of random integers, the occurrence of these integers be equally probable in each given situation. (2) The try-again process is a reasonably efficient procedure. (3) It is actually a closer simulation of actual composing procedures than the "discard" method, since a composer does precisely this. He tries again until a note fits, and if this fails to work, only then does he go back and erase some of his completed work. This is a major point of comparison between what the machine is capable of doing and what a composer normally does. (4) Random search for a note solving the difficulty that calls out the try-again process seems to us to be a more satisfactory method than another possible alternative, the systematic examination of all available notes in a specified order. It is questionable how much the systematic generation of notes would speed up the composition process, since the gain obtained by eliminating repeated tries would be balanced at least in part by the loss suffered by never striking the solution by good fortune ahead of sequence. There is, moreover, a more serious objection than this to systematic note search, namely, that it leads to the weighting of possible solutions depending on the order in which the notes are generated. In addition, it does not yield as readily to theoretical analysis, since it utilizes an already highly organized starting point for further operations rather than one characterized by minimum order.

The Problem of Computer Printout. A practical problem of a different nature is the question of computer output. There are two basic aspects of this problem to be considered: the first being the question of direct printout in musical notation in score form; the second, the direct production of sound, a problem we shall consider in Chapter 7. The practical advantage of having a method for preparing musical printout is only too obvious, for a deficiency of the work to be reported was the necessity of transcribing the results to standard musical notation. The printed output from the Illiac in these experiments was strictly a makeshift in which we utilized presently available Teletype equipment. Although a simple numerical representation used in the earlier experiments was replaced by a letter notation and while we also managed to set up an intelligible representation of rhythms and dynamics, these remained a basically clumsy set of symbols. A number of solutions of this problem appear possible, such as activating a typewriter with musical typeface and appropriate spacing controls. One such typewriter already on the market is the Musicwriter, manufactured by the Music Print Corporation, in Denver, Colorado. This typewriter, however, is a mechanical rather than an electrical typewriter, which causes difficulties when attempting automatic control by means of tape readers or punched-card readers. It should be noted, as also mentioned in Chapter 7, that we are currently undertaking the assembly of a printout unit in cooperation with Cecil Effinger, the designer of the Musicwriter. This will be a musical typewriter controlled by five-channel punched tape of the type used for input and output with the Illiac. In addition, we are currently doing the coding for the Illiac which will permit this unit to be activated properly.

At the time of writing, we have also noticed in the literature that interest in the problem of printout of musical notation is not confined to our own project. From the recent article in *Computing News* previously referred to in Chapter 3,[29] we should like to quote the following passage to illustrate another approach to the same problem:

There is no technical reason that a computer cannot accept the note and octave statements in alphabetical, or other convenient form, and that it cannot produce printed sheet music as an output. The plotting version of the Univac printer (see *Computing News, 104*) is capable of putting out acceptable sheet music in its present version, as is the plotting version of the IBM 407 tabulator (see *Computing News, 100,* page 4).

[29] Anon., "Music Transposition by Computer," *Computing News,* 5(17):108–113, Sept. 1, 1957.

CHAPTER FIVE

Experimental Details

Outline of Experiments

The central body of work, exclusive of the brief preliminary examination of the statistics of the note-selection process discussed in the last chapter, can be grouped into four principal "Experiments." In Experiment One, the two major objectives were (1) to develop a technique for the composition of a simple but recognizable type of melody and (2) to achieve simple polyphonic writing. This second objective, in particular, seemed an essential prerequisite to further experimentation of the type contemplated. Strict counterpoint was selected as the musical medium for Experiment One, which then consisted of three computer programs designed to produce successively monody, two-part writing, and, lastly, four-part writing. However, only a limited number of counterpoint rules were employed, and note selection was confined to the white notes of the C-major scale. This was done to simplify the coding in this initial experiment. Therefore, in the first part of Experiment One, a program was written to permit the writing of simple *cantus firmus* melodies varying from three to twelve notes in length. Then, two-part writing was studied in order to investigate the coding of simple contrapuntal relationships. A number of new problems arose—vertical or chordal relationships, contrary and parallel motion, the rejection of dissonances, and the formation of a simple cadence in C at the end of each *cantus firmus* setting. Lastly, in the third part of this experiment, we were concerned primarily with three-way and four-way note interactions and, in general, with the problem of organizing a much more complex texture and sequence of operations.

At this juncture, it became apparent that all the important remaining rules of counterpoint should be added to the computer code in order to demonstrate more clearly that a recognizable type of music could be produced by computational techniques. Therefore, in what we shall call Experiment Two, a completely rewritten code was prepared to permit the generation of essentially correct four-part first-species counterpoint. This code was so designed that the rules could be added or removed from the set of instructions by simple alterations in the code. Musical output was generated which included examples of settings from purely random white-note writing, obeying no rules whatsoever, to the most restricted settings, in which the full set of rules were applied.

One possible way to continue from this point would have been to proceed to second-species counterpoint—two-against-one writing, rhythmically —then to third species, to fourth species, and eventually to florid counterpoint. In so doing, we would duplicate the experience of a music-theory student, and new and important musical problems such as elementary rhythms, weak and strong beats, and the resolution of dissonances would be introduced in a systematic way. However, it was apparent that this would involve a long process of code writing which, when completed, would still only result in an imitation of one historical musical style. Moreover, it was evident that other types of codes might provide more effective computer methods for various technical problems of music writing and, in particular, for writing music of greater contemporary stylistic interest than strict counterpoint. Therefore, in the first part of Experiment Three, a method was devised for generating independently for each voice rhythmic patterns, dynamic markings, and an index of playing instructions for stringed instruments, such as *legato, staccato, pizzicato,* and *sul ponticello.* This last is an elementary prototype for the more general problem of orchestration. Secondly, the problem of generating the tones to be played was reexamined. Our system was expanded to include the complete chromatic scale rather than just white notes. Initially we generated purely random chromatic music in order to have examples of the most chaotic starting tonal materials, that is, materials of the highest entropy content within the framework of the chromatic scale. Then, in the third part of this third experiment, we modified the rhythm, dynamics, and playing-instructions code so that each of these might pertain to more than one voice at a time, and thus no longer leave the coincidence of rhythm, dynamics, and color effects entirely to chance. Subsequently, this code was combined with the random-note code to provide rhythmic randomly pitched music.

The next step was to restrict the selection of notes somewhat and to give some coherence to the melodic lines. To this end several simple rules were used: (1) a rather special type of octave-range rule; (2) a rule involving the stepwise resolution of tritones to consonant intervals; and (3) a "skip-stepwise" type of melodic rule. This music was generated and then combined with the previously described code for rhythm, dynamics, and playing instructions to produce a texture freely chromatic and dissonant in style, and yet obviously under greater control than purely random output. Since all of these musical examples turned out, as expected, to be highly reminiscent, in terms of over-all sound, of certain styles of contemporary music writing, we completed this Experiment Three by developing a simple technique for generating twelve-tone rows and certain similar restrictive structural devices of current interest.

Experiments of this type, however, soon lead to the asking of whether there are formal principles of organization more general than the various rules of composition involving harmony, counterpoint, and similar techniques. This question formed the basis of studies which have been grouped together as Experiment Four. Since the technical procedure used to produce music by means of the computer was the application of the principles of Markoff processes, it was decided to generate what can be called *Markoff chain music*. A series of studies was undertaken to produce a number of examples of such music. To this end we defined two sets of numbers for assigning values to both absolute and conditional transition probabilities for successive note selection. One set of values was based on the overtone series and permitted the assignment of probabilities for melodic intervals related to their order of occurrence in the harmonic series and, hence, to their relative degrees of consonance. The second set of numbers was used to extend the idea of a leading-tone function. These values were used to control the relative proportions of larger and smaller melodic intervals. Transition probabilities derived from these two sets of integers were combined in various ways to produce melodic output in which the proportion and character of skips and stepwise motions, the proportion of consonant to dissonant intervals, and the resolution of dissonant to consonant textures, or vice versa, were controlled by rather simple means. This last experiment was completed by applying the concept of Markoff chain transition probabilities to the problem of writing an extended cadence, specifically a generalized I–IV–V–I (tonic-subdominant-dominant-tonic) cadence in C.

An outline of the experiments carried out to produce the *Illiac Suite* is given in Table 4. This is also a chronological record of work carried out from September, 1955, through November, 1956.

Experiment One

The logic used to write a computer program differs from the logic one might ordinarily use to explain compositional problems in strictly musical terms. In planning a computer program, the first step is to design a block diagram which outlines the required logical processes. This is followed by the actual writing of the program itself. To illustrate this process, it is convenient to consider the planning of the program for four-part first-species counterpoint, the musical form subject to investigation in the last part of Experiment One and in Experiment Two. This arrangement also permits us to discuss the details of Experiment One rather sketchily since all the significant aspects of coding developed for Experiment One were later refined and incorporated into the more complex set of instructions developed for Experiment Two. In both experiments the same basic musical technique, namely, strict counterpoint, was employed. The pertinent coding details discussed under Experiment Two may, therefore, be considered to apply to Experiment One as well, though, of course, with appropriate simplifications.

Rules of Strict Counterpoint. The method of strict counterpoint was formalized for pedagogical purposes in the *Gradus ad Parnassum,* originally published in 1725 by J. J. Fux,[1] who systematically codified the compositional practices of Palestrina, in Fux's time the best-known composer of the highly consonant polyphonic style of the sixteenth century. Apparently, as disclosed in more recent studies,[2] it seems that Fux allowed some eighteenth-century practices to enter into his method. However, regardless

[1] J. J. Fux, *Steps to Parnassus* (trans. and ed. by A. Mann, with the collaboration of J. St. Edwards), W. W. Norton & Company, Inc., New York, 1943.

[2] K. Jeppeson, *Counterpoint* (trans. by G. Haydon), Prentice-Hall, Inc., Englewood Cliffs, N.J., 1939. See especially ix–xvi and pp. 1–53.

Table 4
Illiac Suite Experiments Summarized

Experiment One: Monody, two-part, and four-part writing

A limited selection of first-species counterpoint rules used for controlling the musical output

    (*a*) Monody: *cantus firmi* 3 to 12 notes in length

    (*b*) Two-part *cantus firmus* settings 3 to 12 notes in length

    (*c*) Four-part *cantus firmus* settings 3 to 12 notes in length

Experiment Two: Four-part first-species counterpoint

Counterpoint rules were added successively to random white-note music as follows:

    (*a*) Random white-note music

    (*b*) Skip-stepwise rule; no more than one successive repeat

    (*c*) Opening C chord; *cantus firmus* begins and ends on C; cadence on C; B–F tritone only in VII$_6$ chord; tritone resolves to C–E

    (*d*) Octave-range rule

    (*e*) Consonant harmonies only except for $\frac{6}{4}$ chords

    (*f*) Dissonant melodic intervals (seconds, sevenths, tritones) forbidden

    (*g*) No parallel unisons, octaves, fifths

    (*h*) No parallel fourths, no $\frac{6}{4}$ chords, no repeat of climax in highest voice

Experiment Three: Experimental music

Rhythm, dynamics, playing instructions, and simple chromatic writing

    (*a*) Basic rhythm, dynamics, and playing-instructions code

    (*b*) Random chromatic music

    (*c*) Random chromatic music combined with modified rhythm, dynamics, and playing-instructions code

    (*d*) Chromatic music controlled by an octave-range rule, a tritone-resolution rule, and a skip-stepwise rule

    (*e*) Controlled chromatic music combined with modified rhythm, dynamics, and playing-instructions code

    (*f*) Interval rows, tone rows, and restricted tone rows

Experiment Four: Markoff chain music

    (*a*) Variation of zeroth-order harmonic probability function from complete tonal restriction to "average" distribution

    (*b*) Variation of zeroth-order harmonic probability function from random to "average" distribution

    (*c*) Zeroth-order harmonic and proximity probability functions and functions combined additively

    (*d*) First-order harmonic and proximity probability functions and functions combined additively

    (*e*) Zeroth-order harmonic and proximity functions on strong and weak beats, respectively, and vice-versa

    (*f*) First-order harmonic and proximity functions on strong and weak beats, respectively, and vice-versa

    (*g*) *i*th-order harmonic function on strong beats, first-order proximity function on weak beats; extended cadence; simple closed form

of how true this is, the rules of strict counterpoint still remain a logical abstraction of many important elements of musical structure and form a fundamental basis for handling linear melodic flow.

Basically, the writing of strict counterpoint involves composing first a *cantus firmus*—a whole-note melody of up to some twelve notes in length. Against this *cantus firmus,* there are set one, two, three, and occasionally more countermelodies. Fux divided counterpoint settings into five "species," in order to introduce compositional problems systematically. In first-species counterpoint, only note-against-note writing is permitted. In second and third species, one or more of the secondary voices moves faster, thus introducing new problems such as weak and strong rhythmic beats and passing-note dissonances. In fourth species, syncopated writing and the resolution of suspensions are treated; while in fifth-species, or florid, counterpoint, all of these techniques are combined. In our discussion, however, we shall be concerned with first species only, since only this type of counterpoint has been programmed in detail for the computer.

The rules derived from first-species counterpoint as used for computer programming may be grouped conveniently into three categories, namely: (1) melodic rules, (2) harmonic or vertical rules, and (3) combined rules. It may be observed that the most important departure from the authentic rules of first-species strict counterpoint is found in the treatment of the cadence. The various rules are also illustrated in Figure 2.

Melodic Rules

1. No melodic line may span more than an octave, i.e., the range from the lowest note to the highest note of a given melodic line should be an octave or less. The limits were set as any octave from the octave C–C' to the octave C'–C", as shown in the first part of Figure 2.

2. If the melodic line is the *cantus firmus* itself, it must begin and end on the tonic. C was selected arbitrarily as the tonic in our experiments.

3. If the melodic line is not the *cantus firmus,* it still must begin and end on notes of the tonic chord. This was the C-major triad in our experiments.

4. A melodic skip of a major or minor seventh is forbidden because this is a dissonant melodic interval.

5. Any melodic skip, i.e., a melodic movement of a minor third or more, must be followed by a tone repeat or by a stepwise motion with or without a change of direction. A stepwise motion is a minor or major second. A stepwise melodic movement may be followed by another stepwise motion

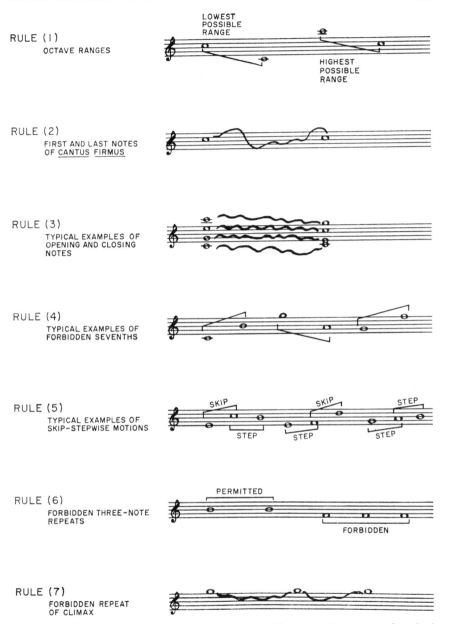

RULE (1)
OCTAVE RANGES

RULE (2)
FIRST AND LAST NOTES
OF CANTUS FIRMUS

RULE (3)
TYPICAL EXAMPLES OF
OPENING AND CLOSING
NOTES

RULE (4)
TYPICAL EXAMPLES OF
FORBIDDEN SEVENTHS

RULE (5)
TYPICAL EXAMPLES OF
SKIP-STEPWISE MOTIONS

RULE (6)
FORBIDDEN THREE-NOTE
REPEATS

RULE (7)
FORBIDDEN REPEAT
OF CLIMAX

Figure 2. The rules of first-species counterpoint illustrated by means of typical musical examples.

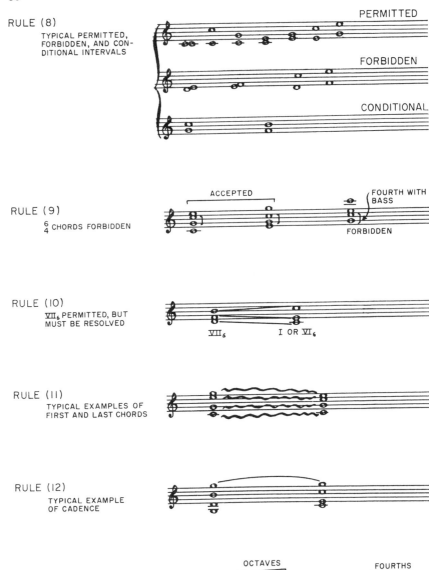

Figure 2. (Continued.)

RULE (14)
PERMITTED PARALLEL
MOTIONS

RULE (15)
REQUIRED STEPWISE
MOTION

RULE (16)
REQUIRED CONTRARY
MOTION

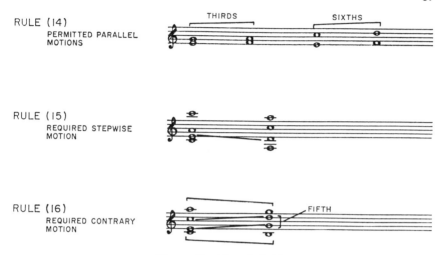

Figure 2. (Concluded.)

or by a skip. It should be noted that this skip-stepwise rule prevents the melodic line from outlining triads.

6. No more than one successive repeat of a given note is permitted.

7. It is forbidden to repeat the highest, or climax, note of a given melodic line unless it is high C and the melodic line happens to move in a tritone resolution or in the cadence up to high C. In our coding, this rule was applied only to the top voice (Violin I).

Harmonic Rules

8. Only consonant intervals are permitted. The permissible intervals include unisons, octaves, perfect fifths, and major and minor thirds and sixths. Forbidden dissonant intervals include major and minor seconds and sevenths, and the tritone, except as under Rule 10 below. By tritone, we refer throughout to both the augmented fourth and diminished fifth, which technically should be distinguished.

9. The perfect fourth is considered a consonance only if it *does not* occur between an upper voice and the voice sounding the lowest note of a chord. This would yield a triad in second inversion (a $\frac{6}{4}$ chord) which is considered dissonant. This rule automatically screens out all perfect fourths in two-part writing.

10. The tritone is considered a dissonant interval, but it is permitted if it occurs in a VII$_6$ chord in major (II$_6$ in minor). The only tritone occurring in C-major *cantus firmus* settings is the B–F interval, which is, there-

fore, permitted if D occurs below the interval. Moreover, the tritone must resolve to the minor sixth E–C, or major third C–E.

11. The first and last chords of a *cantus firmus* setting must be based on the tonic triad. This is a consequence of the second and third melodic rules. Moreover, the lowest notes of these chords must be the tonic itself. Thus, these chords must be in root position.

12. In the cadence (the last two chords of a *cantus firmus* setting) the chord just before the final chord must contain the leading tone B in any one of the four voices, but in not more than one voice. Moreover, this leading tone must move to the tonic. The other counterpoint rules also apply to the cadence. It should be observed that this is a somewhat more liberal cadence rule than that required in traditional strict counterpoint in which the next note to the last of the *cantus firmus* is required to be the supertonic D for settings in C. Actually, this more liberalized cadence formula was more difficult to program than the stricter rule would have been, but we felt that it was a more challenging problem and would produce more interesting cadences.

Combined Rules

13. Parallel unisons, parallel perfect fifths and perfect fourths, and parallel octaves are forbidden.

14. Parallel thirds and sixths are permitted, including parallel major thirds and minor sixths forbidden in the strictest counterpoint.

15. In proceeding from one chord to the next, at least one of the four voices must move by stepwise motion or remain stationary.

16. If any two voices move in the same direction into a unison, perfect fifth, perfect fourth, or octave, then one of the remaining voices must move by contrary stepwise motion or stay on the same note.

Processing These Rules for Coding. Upon examination of these rules of counterpoint, it was evident that, for setting up computer operations to be outlined by means of a block diagram, these rules could be classified as follows: (1) where voices are considered one at a time, (2) where voices are considered two at a time, (3) where voices are considered four at a time. Class 1 includes all of the melodic rules; class 2 includes all the rules designed to exclude harmonic dissonance; and class 3 includes more complicated rules such as having at least one voice moving in contrary motion in respect to others.

Secondly, it was observed that the over-all selection of notes could be divided into three classes of operation as follows: (1) initial notes, (2) intermediate notes, and (3) cadence notes. Thirdly, while it was entirely possible to generate all the intermediate-type notes randomly and reject those which do not satisfy the rules, it was also observed that, for the sake of efficiency, it was possible to reduce the rejection rate considerably by establishing three basic subclasses of intermediate notes as follows: (1) tritone-resolution notes, (2) skip-stepwise notes, and (3) random notes. In subclass 1, the notes to be used were predetermined by the fact that a tritone would have occurred which requires a particular resolution. In such a circumstance, the generation of random notes would have been wasteful, and it was far simpler to supply the required notes directly. Subclass 2 notes were required whenever a melodic skip occurred. Here again, it would have been simply wasteful to generate random notes, and it was more efficient to restrict the note selection to the few possible choices. Since there are permitted only two possible stepwise motions plus the repeat of a note, it was convenient to generate randomly one of the three increments −1, 0, +1 equivalent to these melodic intervals and add it to the previous note. Subclass 3 notes, that is, all other intermediate notes, were generated purely randomly.

The Try-again Subroutine. Whenever a note was rejected, another note to replace it had to be generated and tested. To do this, insertion of the try-again subroutine, described in the last chapter, into the counterpoint program was required. A count was kept of the number of times the computer tried again, and if, after a sufficient number of trials, the probability of all the possible notes being tested at least once was very high and the notes were still being rejected, the computer was instructed to erase from storage the "composition" thus far completed and start all over again. As already noted in Chapter 4, the number of trials was set at fifty by a simple counting index.

A "Direction of Composition." If we define the term the direction of composition as the sequence chosen for placing notes successively in a musical composition, then we observe that a direction of composition is required the moment two-part and four-part writing is initiated. In this type of writing, in the experiments to be described, the direction of composition was set as one *harmonic line,* that is, one *vertical line,* musically, at a time. This sequence of note selection seemed to us to be a somewhat more practical and efficient method than the alternate procedure of composing initially a complete *cantus firmus* and then attempting to find other mutually compatible melodic lines which could be set against this *cantus firmus.* It should be emphasized, however, that this alternate method could have been employed had we so desired. Therefore, the actual "composing procedure" adopted was the following for four-part counterpoint: A note of the *cantus firmus*, or Voice 1 (cello), was generated first and then followed successively by the generation of notes for Voice 2 (viola), for Voice 3 (violin II), and lastly for Voice 4 (violin I), except in special situations such as tritone resolutions and cadences in which some voices were already determined.

Indexing the Notes of the Scale. As already noted, for the generation of first-species counterpoint, it was possible to restrict the choice of notes to the white notes of the scale, since C-major *cantus firmus* settings were being considered. This was a desirable simplification, since it reduced the number of random notes which needed to be generated. Hence, efficiency was increased and the complexity of the program was reduced. The notes of the musical scale were therefore indexed in simple numerical sequences upwards from low C, omitting the sharps and flats, as shown in Figure 3.

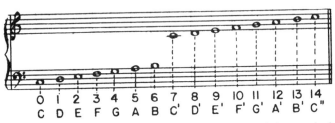

Figure 3. Numerical index of the white notes of the musical scale as used in Experiments One and Two.

It should be mentioned that starting the index with the number 0 rather than 1 is a convenience for setting up arithmetical operations in the computer. Otherwise, this somewhat unusual method of numbering has no significance. It might also be noted that the output produced in both Experiments One and Two was printed in number notation on the Teletype machine in accord with the index shown in Figure 3. Transcription of this notation to standard musical notation was then carried out by hand.

In assigning integers in this way to represent the notes of the musical scale, it should be clear that we did not adopt some completely arbitrary procedure. In Experiments One and Two, we preserved the same order in this numerical—or stochastic—representation as that of the musical scale. Moreover, as we shall see later on in Experiment Three, when we revised this representation to apply to the ordinary chromatic scale, the numerical difference between any two of these stochastic representations corresponded to the number of half-tone steps separating the notes being represented. Thus, numerical representations became associated with particular musical intervals. It was this fact which enabled us to add the number representing an interval to a previous note and thereby produce the correct numerical representation of a new note. With these basic decisions made, it was then possible to sketch block diagrams for each of the parts of Experiment One.

Simple Monody: Coding for *Cantus Firmi.* In this first part of Experiment One, we limited the control over the musical materials to the same rules used in the preliminary tests before the try-again subroutine was developed, namely: (1) no melodic sevenths, (2) no melodic tritones, (3) the octave-range rule, and (4) the rule that all the *cantus firmi* must start and end on C. A comparison of these few rules with the counterpoint rules listed earlier disclosed that many violations of the technique of strict counterpoint could be anticipated, and indeed, as we shall see, the results showed that all possibilities not specifically excluded by the rules employed appeared in the musical output.

The actual computer program was similar to the "melodic subroutine" to be described under Experiment Two and included in addition a simple program for fixing the first and last notes as C. The lengths of the *cantus firmi* were set by a simple counter. Thus for a *cantus firmus* containing n notes, this counter was set at $-n+1$, and after each note was selected (including the first note), unity was added to this quantity to yield the successive values $-n+2$, $-n+3$, . . . , $-n+n$. This last value, occurring after note $n-1$ had been selected, is, of course, equal numerically to zero, the lowest possible positive number recognized in computer calculations. The change in sign from a series of negative numbers to a positive number was detected by a conditional transfer order, which was then used to shift to the instructions used to terminate the *cantus firmus* with the note C and begin a new *cantus firmus.* The number of *cantus firmi* of each given length was controlled by another counter working on the same simple principle. Lastly, the lengths of the various *cantus firmi*, denoted by the function n, were obtained by means of a series of preselected stored parameters used for n.

In the first run, it was decided to generate fifty samples each of *cantus firmi* from three to twelve notes long to produce a total of five hundred of these simple melodies. The actual time required to do this in the computer was limited primarily by the time the computer required to punch the output tape.

Simple Two-part *Cantus Firmus* Settings. The next step was to consider simple two-part writing in which some vertical relationships between the two voices had to be considered and yet in which the complications involved in crosschecking more complex relationships between more than two voices were still avoided. Therefore, for the new added voice, the same melodic rules as used for the *cantus firmus* were put in effect, except that the first notes were permitted to be E or G as well as C. Secondly, vertical dissonances, specifically seconds and sevenths, the B–F tritone, and perfect fourths, were forbidden in what was to become eventually the "harmonic subroutine" of Experiment Two. Thirdly, as a simple cadence subroutine, it was required that a leading tone B be inserted in either one of the two voices in the next-to-last chord and that this B resolve upwards to C. The selection of which voice the B was made to occur in was carried out by means of a binary random-choice operation and was also made to depend upon proper voice leading, in accord with the rules in effect. Fourthly, parallel unisons, octaves, and fifths occurring between successive chords were forbidden. The technique for accomplishing this in four-part writing is described under Experiment Two. Again, as in the case of the *cantus firmi* alone, fifty each of *cantus firmus* settings from three to twelve notes long were produced.

Simple Four-part *Cantus Firmus* Settings. In the last part of Experiment One, we extended our technique to include four voices, in accord with the primary objective of this experiment. The principal problem now became one of dealing with a set of interactions of increased complexity. In this first attempt at four-part writing, we still kept the rules relatively simple and added as few new rules of operation as possible beyond those used for two-part settings. Certain operations were actually liberalized; specifically, $\frac{6}{4}$ chords and the VII$_6$ chord were permitted. As it turned out, two sets of computations were completed in this last part of Experiment One. The results of the first set indicated that, even at this point, the attrition because of the restrictions already in effect was so great that certain undesirable results were occurring very frequently. Specifically, the most objectionable result was the occurrence of many repeats of a given note in the same voice. It turned out that many reiterations of one note became a convenient solution to many of the voice-leading problems which arose in this style of counterpoint. While not necessarily unattractive in sound, this was, for our purposes, an undesirable end result. Hence, for a second run, an additional rule was inserted into the program to forbid more than one successive repeat of any note.

The increase in complexity which resulted as a consequence of four-part writing involved the problem that all the harmonic and parallel-motion rules had to be cross-checked between all voices. Thus, six separate cross checks were written into the computer instructions. These were required for the following pairs: Voice 1–Voice 2, Voice 1–Voice 3, Voice 1–Voice 4, Voice 2–Voice 3, Voice 2–Voice 4, and Voice 3–Voice 4. This became the entry of the "harmonic subroutine" of Experiment Two, which had to be entered six times in order that all the voices were properly cross-checked.

Lastly, a routine for the cadence formula, listed as Rule 12, had to be written. This turned out to be a complicated problem in itself. In this routine, described fully under Experiment Two, all the standard voice-leading and harmonic rules still had to be checked, but there were, as well, additional restrictions defining acceptable note combinations. The cadence routine was in essence a program which contained instructions embodying these additional restrictions and also a long series of rewrite orders which temporarily rewrote large sections of the regular counterpoint instructions so that they might be specifically applied to the cadence formula.

As in the previous parts of Experiment One, fifty samples each of settings from three to twelve notes long were produced.

Experiment Two

With the basic points considered under the topic of Experiment One in mind, it is now possible in discussing the details of Experiment Two to examine some block diagrams actually used in the production of musical materials in Experiment Two. It is convenient to start with the diagram for the main routine shown in Figure 4.

Main Routine for Four-part First-species Counterpoint. In the upper left-hand corner of the diagram shown in Figure 4, there is a box labeled "Initial Entry," which represents the routine instructions carried out directly after the program is read into the computer. This block includes routine operations such as clearing storage locations, setting up indices and counters, storing parameters, and so on. It is at this point that instructions for the number of *cantus firmus* settings of various lengths to be completed in each given computer run were included in this particular program of instructions.

Initial Notes Subroutine.[3] Following these preliminaries, the first im-

---

[3] The term *subroutine* in our discussion is not restricted to the self-contained group of orders with a formalized entry and exit, sometimes more precisely called a *closed subroutine*. Both open and closed subroutines were used in this programming depending upon circumstances and convenience.

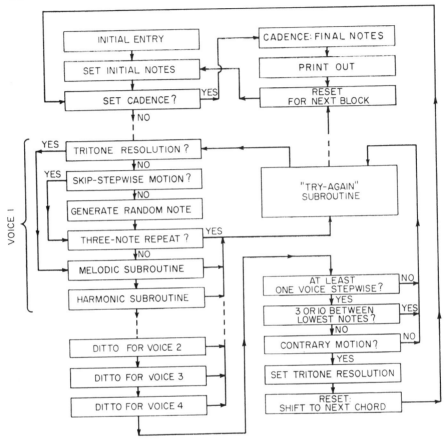

Figure 4. Experiment Two: Block diagram for the main routine.

portant task was to set the first chord of the first *cantus firmus* setting in accord with Rules 2, 3, and 11, given on pages 84 and 88. This was done by means of a special subroutine required only at the beginning of each *cantus firmus* setting. Once it had been used, this subroutine was not entered again until after a setting had been completed and the computer was ready to proceed with the generation of the next setting.

The basic problem was to set the chord of C major *in root position* into the four voices in the most efficient manner. Since only the notes C, E, G, C′, E′, G′, and C″, with numerical equivalents of 0, 2, 4, 7, 9, 11, and 14, respectively, were involved, it was possible to restrict the choice of random integers to these few numbers by storing these particular numbers in a special small table of seven entries and selecting the memory locations for these numbers by random-integer generation, utilizing the technique already described in Chapter 4. Moreover, since the initial note for the *cantus firmus* (Voice 1) was limited even more to just C, C′, or C″, to make the note-selection process as simple as possible, we could arbitrarily select C′, for which the numerical equivalent is 7, for this voice. This automatically ensured that the chord would be in root position, since Voice 1, being for the cello, would subsequently be transposed downward an octave.

Main Routine Continued. Since *cantus firmus* settings from as short as three notes to any reasonable length might be required, the next logical step was to ask whether the next-to-last chord had been reached and whether the cadence routine would be required. This would happen immediately, of course, only when the length of the setting had been restricted to three notes. However, it was desirable that this decision be made at this point because of the cyclic nature of the program. In the experiments actually carried out with the Illiac, the longest settings generated were twelve notes long, and all the output for Experiment Two, in particular, was limited to this length. However, this was not the case in Experiment One, as we have already seen. This decision operation, which not only brought the special cadence routine into operation, but also set the lengths of the *cantus firmus* settings, worked in the following way: If we wished to write settings for *cantus firmi* n notes long, a cadence routine would be required after $n-2$ notes had been generated in each voice, since both the last and next-to-last chords would be involved in the cadence. Therefore, the number $-(n-2)$ could be set in a convenient storage location, and after each chord was successfully completed, a unit increment could be added to this quantity to obtain successively the values $-(n-3)$, $-(n-4)$, . . . , -1, 0, as shown in Table 5. Again since zero is considered a positive number, when the operation $-(n-2) + (n-2)$ was carried out after $n-2$ chords had been formed, a change of sign took place. This change of sign activated the conditional transfer order and caused the sequence of operations to shift to the special cadence routine. Until this change of sign occurred, however, the transfer order was bypassed and the principal part of the program, which was used for the generation of intermediate notes, was entered.

The next group of six blocks of instructions bracketed as referring to Voice 1 was repeated with minor variations also for Voices 2, 3, and 4, taken successively. These were blocks of instructions primarily derived from rules for the voices taken one at a time or two at a time. In fact, these

Table 5
Experiment Two
Counting Operation for Activating the Cadence Routine

Last chord formed	Index plus counter		Effect on conditional transfer order to cadence
Initial chord	$-(n-2)$	$= -(n-2) + 0 = -(n-2)$	*Negative numbers*
Second chord	$-(n-2) + 1$	$= -(n-2) + 1 = -(n-3)$	Do not set cadence
Third chord	$-(n-3) + 1$	$= -(n-2) + 2 = -(n-4)$	Do not transfer
	$-(n-4) + 1$	$= -(n-2) + 3 = -(n-5)$	Continue with main routine
.	.	.	
.	.	.	
.	.	.	
$(n-3)$rd chord	$-(n-n+2) + 1 = -(n-2) + (n-3) = -1$		
$(n-2)$nd chord	$-(n-n+1) + 1 = -(n-2) + (n-2) = 0$		*Positive number*
			Transfer to cadence routine

operations took care of all of the rules for intermediate notes except some of the more complex interactions which could only be tested for after all four notes were selected.

Within the group of instructions for each voice, the two special types of notes which could be set without resorting to the general random note scheme were treated first. In the set of more general instructions—on the right-hand side of Figure 4—the block labeled "Set Tritone Resolution" is a set of instructions which was activated whenever a tritone—which in these experiments was limited to the combinations F–B, F–B', B–F', F'–B'—had occurred between any two voices in the previous chord. The "Set Tritone Resolution" operation also recorded between which voices the tritone had occurred and stored this information for the "Tritone Resolution" block for Voices 1, 2, 3, and 4. Lastly, it also eliminated tritones occurring between more than two voices, which could arise only as a consequence of doubling at the unison or octave. These doublings were unacceptable, since they would produce forbidden parallel motions at the unison or octave. It should also be noted that before the tritone-resolution notes were set for the next chord, they were examined by means of the melodic subroutine to be described below. If they were found to be unacceptable, the chord was erased and started over.

The tritone-resolution operation was used therefore, whenever a tritone had occurred between two voices only, and only when one of the tritone-interval notes had occurred in the voice for which a new note was being generated. If the tritone note in the previous chord happened to have been F or F' (index numbers 3 or 10) or B or B' (index numbers 6 or 13), the notes in the new chord were automatically inserted as E or E' (2 or 9) or C or C' (7 or 14), respectively. Otherwise, the operation was bypassed.

The skip-stepwise operation was based upon Rule 3 and was set up so as to be more efficient than testing randomly generated notes for Rule 3. The two notes previous to the one being generated were first examined by finding the negative absolute value of the difference of their values. Thus, if we were about to generate note N_i, we computed $-|N_{i-1} - N_{i-2}|$. The quantity 1 was then added to this value, and if the result turned out to be positive, we knew that the previous melodic interval had been smaller than a third, that is, it had been a stepwise motion. The positive sign, if it occurred, was used to activate the conditional transfer order, this time to bypass the special skip-stepwise routine and to proceed to the generation of a random note. On the other hand, if the number was found to be negative, we simply generated at random the values $+1$, 0, or -1 for the interval $N_i - N_{i-1}$, bypassed the general random-note-generation process, and proceeded to further testing. This calculation is illustrated in Table 6.

Table 6
Experiment Two
An Illustration of the Process for Detecting Skips in
Applying the Skip-stepwise Rule

Note N_{i-1}	Note N_{i-2}	$-\lvert N_{i-1} - N_{i-2} \rvert$	$-\lvert N_{i-1} - N_{i-2} \rvert + 1$
C'(7)	C'(7)	0	+1 ⎱ *Stepwise motion*
A(5)	B(6)	−1	0 ⎰ Generate random note
E'(9)	G'(11)	−2	−1 ⎱ *Skip*
C"(14)	G'(11)	−3	−2 ⎸ Generate +1, 0, or −1
etc.			. ⎸ for the interval,
			. ⎸ $N_i - N_{i-1}$
			. ⎸
			. ⎰

To generate the increments +1, 0, and −1, we simply used the random-integer-generation process previously described in Chapter 4, setting $b = 3$ to yield the values 0, 1, and 2 in random sequence. By subtracting 1 from these values, we obtained in turn −1, 0, and +1 in random sequence.

The next step in the process was the generation of a random note without restriction. Since there were fifteen possible notes available for selection, n was set at 17, this being the smallest prime number above 15, and the integers 15 and 16, whenever they turned up, were rejected by means of the process of the type shown in Table 7.

The next step was the elimination of multiple repeats of the same note, specifically, the elimination of all repeats of the same note but one. To do this, the quantity $\lvert N_i - N_{i-1} \rvert$ was first computed, and if it was found to be unequal to zero, the test was concluded, since this meant that the previous melodic interval had *not* been a repeat. On the other hand, if the difference was found to be zero, then further testing for the second interval back was also required. The interval $\lvert N_{i-1} - N_{i-2} \rvert$ was then computed. If this was found to be unequal to zero, we know the second melodic interval back had *not* been a repeat. In this case, the test was again concluded. However, if this difference was also found to be zero, then two repeats in a row had occurred. Since this is forbidden by the rules, the generated note, in this case, had to be rejected and try-again subroutine entered.

Melodic Subroutine. The melodic subroutine, which in simplified form, but with additions for selecting the first and last notes of a *cantus firmus*, had been also the first music-generation code written for the Illiac as part

Table 7
Experiment Two
Process for Rejecting Certain Random Integers
(Specifically 15 and 16) Out of the Set, 0, 1, . . . , 16

Random integer	Random integer — 15	Conditional transfer result
0	—15	Accept
1	—14	
.	.	
.	.	
.	.	
.	.	
14	—1	
15	0	Reject and recycle to repeat
16	+1	random-integer generation

of Experiment One, was used both to screen out forbidden intervals between successive notes and to check longer-range interactions between the notes of a given melodic line.

In the testing of intervals between successive notes, a simple additive process was employed. Initially, $|N_i - N_{i-1}|$ was computed and the quantity 7 subtracted from this absolute difference. As shown in Figure 5, each time we tested this yielded one of a series of integers which could then be checked to find the exact magnitude of the melodic interval. Since the only forbidden melodic intervals were sevenths and tritones, only these had to be screened out. Therefore, it was possible to test immediately for whether the interval was an octave or larger, and if so, the interval was conditionally accepted. Since intervals larger than an octave were automatically eliminated by the test to follow for the octave-range rule, the octave was, in effect, being detected by this first screening operation. Directly thereafter, it was possible to test for the seventh. If the seventh was found, the try-again routine was entered, and the whole process started over again. On the other hand, if the seventh was not found, then, by the rules, all the remaining intervals were acceptable except the tritone, and the possibility of the presence of this interval could immediately be tested for. Therefore, a screening operation for sixths could be omitted.

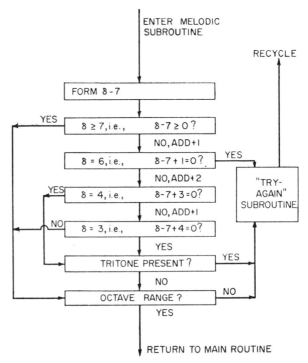

Figure 5.   Experiment Two: Block diagram for the
melodic subroutine.

It was possible to proceed directly to the detection of the presence of fifths
and fourths, that is, of whether $\delta = |N_i - N_{i-1}| = 4$ or 3. If one or the
other of these intervals was found, the presence of a tritone was possibly
indicated and additional screening was required. Thus, if the difference
$\delta = 4$ was found, then a tritone involving the notes B–F′ (indexed as 6
and 10) had to be tested for by a subtractive process. Alternatively, if the
difference $\delta = 3$ was found, the possibility of the existence of one of the
other two different tritone intervals, F–B and F′–B′, had to be checked.
Again, subtractive tests were employed for this purpose. Moreover, the
higher interval F′−B′ was first lowered by an octave, so that the same test
could be employed for both these intervals.

The next operation involved the octave-range rule, Rule 1, which was,
for us, one of the more interesting rules of counterpoint. As noted
previously, this rule states that a melodic line is limited to a span of an
octave or less, but it does not specify which particular octave span this
range must encompass. This operation is in some ways more generalized

than most of the others, for the specific limitations it imposes upon the melody develop only as the melody is being written. Therefore, each time a note was generated, track had to be kept of whether this new note was more than an octave higher or lower than *any other note* already present in the melody. If not, then the note was provisionally accepted and the test concluded. On the other hand, if the note violated this rule by exceeding an octave, then the try-again subroutine was entered. This test operated quite simply as follows: The note just generated, N_i, was subtracted from note N_1. The quantity 8, which is equivalent to the span of a ninth, was then subtracted from the absolute value of this difference, and if the result remained positive, we knew that a skip larger than an octave between this most recent note and the first note of the melodic line had been formed and the note N_i was rejected. This process was then repeated successively for $N_i - N_2$, $N_i - N_3$, to $N_i - N_{i-1}$, and only if the condition required by Rule 1 was fulfilled for all these intervals was the note accepted.

Finally, the repeat of a climax in the melodic line of the highest voice, which, in accord with Rule 7, we considered to be forbidden, was tested for. Although this routine was not a part of the melodic subroutine since it had to be employed only in connection with the highest voice, it is convenient to mention it at this point. As each note in the highest voice was accepted, a record was kept of the highest note generated up to that point, and a specific test was eventually made of whether a repeat of this note had occurred. This rule, however, was not applied in the cadence or in conflict with the tritone-resolution rule.

Harmonic Subroutine. The principal function of this subroutine was to screen out vertical dissonances and to restrict chords to perfect triads and their first inversions, the one chord with a permissible dissonance being VII_6, which contains the tritone interval. The block diagram for this subroutine is shown in Figure 6. In Figure 6, we have used the symbol Δ to represent a vertical interval, that is, the absolute numerical difference between the notes in two different voices on the same beat.

The subroutine has been simplified in Figure 6 to show how the testing is carried out between any two voices, but it should be remembered that the relationships between all possible pairs of voices had to be examined. The six possible combinations of voices taken two at a time are V_1-V_2, V_1-V_3, V_1-V_4, V_2-V_3, V_2-V_4, and V_3-V_4. The harmonic subroutine had, therefore, to be entered a total of six times before a particular combination of notes could be passed as acceptable. It was most efficient to design a

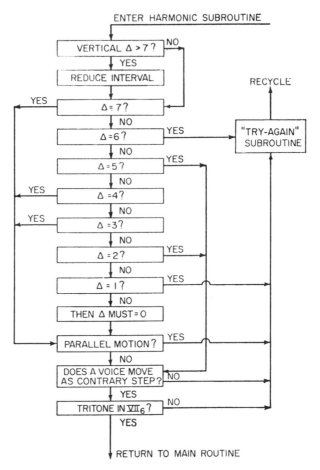

Figure 6. Experiment Two: Block diagram for the
harmonic subroutine.

recycling operation for testing all four voices by means of the melodic and
harmonic subroutines by using a set of indices which would keep track of
what was tested and which would also carry out the testing in the most
efficient manner. The order of testing is shown in Table 8.

The harmonic subroutine was used (1) to eliminate vertical sevenths and
seconds, (2) to eliminate parallel unisons, fourths, fifths, and octaves, all of
which are forbidden by the rules, (3) to test whether a unison, fourth,
fifth, or octave had been formed by the two voices moving in the same direction by contrary stepwise motion, or by one or both voices remaining
stationary, and (4) to test whether a tritone had occurred. The testing of

Table 8
Order of Testing the Four Voices with the
Melodic and Harmonic Subroutines

Voice 1

Enter melodic subroutine for V_1
Harmonic subroutine is not entered since there is nothing to test

Voice 2

Enter melodic subroutine for V_2
Enter harmonic subroutine for $V_1 - V_2$

Voice 3

Enter melodic subroutine for V_3
Enter harmonic subroutine for $V_1 - V_3$, $V_2 - V_3$

Voice 4

Test for repeat of climax note
Enter melodic subroutine for V_4
Enter harmonic subroutine for $V_1 - V_4$, $V_2 - V_4$, $V_3 - V_4$

whether D, rather than B or F, was the lowest note of the one chord which might contain a tritone, that is, of whether the chord was VII_6 and not VII or VII_6, was done later in the main routine after the whole chord being formed had been completed.

Table 9
Experiment Two
Reducing Vertical Interval to an Octave or Less

Interval	Δ	$\Delta - 8$		Reduced Δ		Δ for testing
Double octave	14	6		7		0
Fourteenth	13	5		6		−1
.	.	.		.		.
.	.	.	+1	.		.
.	.	.	⟶	.		.
.	.	.		.		.
.	.	.		.		.
Tenth	9	1		2	−7	−5
Ninth	8	0		1	⟶	−6
Octave	7	−1		7		0
Seventh	6	−2		6		−1
.	.	.	discard	.		.
.	.	.	and use	.		.
.	.	.	original	.		.
Unison	0	−8		0		−7

In order to simplify the testing procedure, all vertical intervals larger than an octave were first reduced. This was accomplished by computing the absolute difference $\Delta = |V_a - V_b|$ and subtracting 8 from the result. If a positive number resulted, we knew from this calculation that the original interval was larger than an octave, and +1 was added to the result to yield the reduced interval. On the other hand, if a negative answer was obtained, the original interval was employed directly for the tests. This calculation is shown in Table 9.

The next step was to eliminate sevenths and seconds and to set up the remaining tests in the subroutine. For convenience in applying the conditional transfer order, 7 was subtracted from these adjusted values of Δ just computed. Sevenths and seconds were first eliminated by adding unity successively to $\Delta - 7$ and, after each addition, testing with the conditional transfer order in order to place the interval into the proper category for subsequent processing. The technique for doing this is shown in Table 10.

In the parallel-motion test, which was applied only when $\Delta = 0$, 3, 4, or 7, Δ_i was compared with Δ_{i-1} to see whether $\Delta_i = \Delta_{i-1}$. Whenever this occurred, we knew forbidden parallel motion had occurred, either actually, as in the examples shown in Figure 7a, or implicitly by octave

Figure 7. Experiment Two: Examples of (a) direct parallel motion, (b) implicit parallel motion.

displacement, as in the examples shown in Figure 7b. The previous interval for the two voices in question, Δ_{i-1}, was obtained from storage and reduced if necessary. It was then directly tested by subtracting from it the quantity Δ_i. If the difference was found to be unequal to zero, we knew immediately that parallel motion had not occurred.

The two remaining tests included with the harmonic subroutine also depended on the examination of the intervals between the voices taken two at a time. In the test for contrary motion, again only applied whenever $\Delta = 0$, 3, 4, or 7, the signs of the differences $N_i - N_{i-1}$ for each of the two voices in question were determined. If the signs were unlike, then con-

Table 10
Experiment Two
Calculations for Testing Vertical Intervals between Pairs of Voices

Interval	Δ	$\Delta - 7$						
Unison	0	−7	−6	−5	−4	−3	−2	−1
Second	1	−6	−5	−4	−3	−2	−1	0
Third	2	−5	−4	−3	−2	−1		
Fourth	3	−4	−3	−2	−1			
Fifth	4	−3	−2	−1				
Sixth	5	−2	−1					
Seventh	6	−1						
Octave	7	0						

+1 → Accept
0 → Reject
+1 → Accept
0 → Accept
+1 → Accept
0 → Accept
+1 → Accept
0 → Accept
+1 → Accept
0 → Accept
−1 → Accept
0 → Reject

Transfer to parallel-motion routine
Transfer to main routine
Transfer to try-again subroutine

trary motion had occurred and the test was concluded, since contrary motion was permissible. But if like signs were found, the two voices had to be tested for whether one or both of them had remained stationary, that is, for whether the value $N_i - N_{i-1} = 0$, which was also permissible as such. Otherwise, it was recorded that a possible violation of Rule 16 was indicated and that further testing in the main routine would be required to determine whether one of the remaining voices had concurrently moved by contrary motion. The testing for sign was done directly by means of the conditional transfer order.

In the last test, the specific reduced interval F–B was first searched for whenever Δ had been found by previous testing to be equal to 3 or 4. This was done by determining whether any of the quantities $N_i - 3$, $N_i - 6$, $N_i - 10$, or $N_i - 13$ equaled zero in each of the two voices to be tested. If so, it was noted that a tritone had occurred, and the rest of the test was then carried out. In the second part of this test, the presence of doubling either at the unison or octave was checked, and if found, the doubling was removed by erasing the chord and starting over again by means of the try-again subroutine. Finally, in a later part of this test, the presence in one of the remaining voices of a D lower than the tritone interval was tested for by first finding the lowest note of the tritone interval and then subtracting from this, successively, the notes in the two remaining voices. If the difference was found to be positive, we knew that a note lower than the interval existed, and we also knew that this note had to be a D, since the notes C and A form dissonant intervals with B, and the notes E and G form dissonant intervals with F.

Main Routine Continued. Once all the tests embodied in the melodic and harmonic subroutines had been successfully passed, the main routine was returned to in order that the notes now provisionally accepted could be screened through tests expressing the rules related to combined interactions between the voices. As shown in Figure 4, there were three tests which had to be satisfied. The first, based on Rule 15, required that at least one voice out of the four be required to move stepwise. This rule was checked rather easily since all that was necessary was that at least one voice be found for which $|N_i - N_{i-1}| = 1$. As soon as this condition was found to be satisfied, the test was concluded and the next operation started. This was the process needed to eliminate $\frac{6}{4}$ chords. The procedure used was the following: The lowest note of the chord was first found by testing whether Voice 1 might happen to have it by subtracting this note from the notes of the chord in Voice 2, Voice 3, and Voice 4, in that order. This process was kept up as long as the difference remained positive. If all these differences did remain positive, it was evident that Voice 1 contained the lowest note of the chord, and this part of the test was concluded. On the other hand, if the difference in any of these subtractions turned out to be negative, we knew that the other voice of the pair being examined contained the lower note, and it was used to replace Voice 1 in subsequent screening for the lowest note. This procedure was repeated until the lowest note was found. The next step after this was to set up a check for whether a difference of 3 or 10 existed between this lowest note and any other of the three other notes. If not, then we knew that a $\frac{6}{4}$ chord had not been formed, and we were able to proceed to the next test, which was the check for contrary motion in at least one voice whenever a unison, perfect fourth, fifth, or octave formed by motion in the same direction had been detected in the harmonic subroutine as described above. Two memory locations were cleared to zero—one for positive increment and one for negative increment for the four melodic intervals between the chord under examination and the previous chord. The four melodic intervals were then computed one at a time. If a given melodic interval was found to be zero, i.e., if it was found to be a melodic repeat, nothing was entered into the two memory locations. On the other hand, if the interval was found to be positive or negative, the appropriate one of the two aforementioned locations was made nonzero. After all four intervals had been processed, both memory locations were tested for nonzero value. The actual magnitudes contained therein did not matter; the important thing to determine was whether only one of the two locations was nonzero. If this condition was found, then no contrary motion had occurred and a new chord had to be generated. On the other hand, if both were nonzero, this showed that the requirement for contrary motion had been satisfied, and we could then immediately proceed to the next operation, which was the setting up of the tritone-resolution process, described earlier, for chords containing a tritone interval.

Lastly, the two "Reset" operations, one for shifting to the next chord of a given *cantus firmus* setting and the other for starting a new setting, were both basically clearing operations for resetting indices back to original values. In addition, the "Reset: Shift to Next Chord" operation also carried out the process of storing the chord formed into the computer memory until the time when it was to be printed out or, alternatively, to be erased as a consequence of the try-again subroutine.

Cadence Routine. As already noted in our discussion of Experiment One, a routine had to be written for the cadence whenever chord $n-2$ was reached, the length of the *cantus firmus* setting being set at n notes. Moreover, in this routine, as observed before, all the standard voice-leading and harmonic rules still had to be checked. In addition, further restrictions embodied in Rules 2, 3, 7, 11, and, in particular, Rule 12 had to be recognized and properly tested for.

There were two basic procedures which were open to us. The first was to write a complete new set of orders which would test for all the rules applicable to the cadence as a self-contained closed subroutine, while the second was to assemble a set of overwrite orders so that we might apply the main routine for the major portions of the *cantus firmus* setting also to the cadence. This latter procedure would require some additional testing procedures for the extra restrictions required by the cadence formula but would eliminate duplication of various standard tests already discussed. For this latter reason, this second procedure was adopted as the preferred one.

In the cadence routine as written, the first step was to place the note B (or B′) in one of the four voices. Two operations were required here. The first was to select either B or B′ by two-choice random-integer generation, while the second was to determine by four-choice random-integer generation into which of the four voices this note was to be inserted. The operations required to check the rules of melodic writing contained in the main routine were then called into play to determine whether the selected note satisfied these rules. If so, the remaining notes of the chord were selected by the ordinary note-selection processes already described and screened for the usual restrictions. In actual fact, this eliminated all chords but V, V_6, III, III_6, and VII_6. In addition, a new test had also to be included to eliminate doubling of the leading tone B, either at the unison or octave. This test was carried out by means of simple subtractive tests of the general type already described.

Once the leading tone chord at position $n-1$ was obtained, the final chord could be selected. Since this had to be a tonic chord in root position just like the initial chord, the subroutine for selecting the initial chord could readily be adapted to this purpose. It was modified, however, to ensure that the leading tone progressed to C, and following this, the remaining notes were generated until an acceptable combination was found. In so doing, the restriction as to the repeat of the highest note of the highest voice was relaxed to the extent that a repeat of C″ occurring on this last chord was permitted if the preceding note happened to have been B′.

The extensive set of rewrite orders required for this cadence subroutine involved the adapting of test procedures from the other parts of the computer program for Experiment Two. A complicated bookkeeping operation was needed to set up the testing procedures for the cadence and to reconstruct the tests in their original form for the next *cantus firmus* setting after the cadence had been selected. The details of these instructions need not be considered here since, although complex, they were entirely routine in nature.

Printout. Printout instructions were activated in the program for Experiment Two whenever a *cantus firmus* setting was completed. The setting was read from the memory and printed by means of standard subroutines available for the Illiac. After printing (actually, after output tape was punched), the memory locations used for storage of the *cantus firmus* setting were cleared, and the resetting of the machine for writing the next sample of counterpoint was initiated. A sample of computer output produced by means of this program is shown in Figure 8.

07	08	05	06	09	09	12	11	09	09	11	09
09	06	07	04	05	02	03	06	05	05	02	09
09	13	12	09	09	12	12	11	12	14	11	11
07	11	12	06	05	09	08	11	12	07	06	07

Figure 8. Experiment Two: Sample of typical printed output in which some counterpoint rules are in effect.

Varying the Number of Rules Used. As noted in the Outline of Experiments and as shown in Table 4, musical output was generated by means of this program to include examples of *cantus firmus* settings in which the number of restrictions were varied from purely random white-note writing, in which no rules whatsoever were applied, to the most restricted writing, in which the full set of instructions was utilized. The various types of settings between these two extremes produced in a series of computer runs are tabulated in Table 4. Actually, the experiments were carried out in reverse order. The most complicated program, the one we have just described, was written first. After this was in working order and producing output, it was then a simple task to reduce its complexity by means of overwrite orders which inserted bypass, or "unconditional transfer orders," into the program in front of the tests to be eliminated. When a sufficient number of these bypass orders had been inserted, the program was reduced to the simple process of generating random white-note music.

In conclusion, it is of interest to note that this was the most complex single music-generation program we have written so far for the Illiac. The total number of individual arithmetical instructions required by this program for writing strict counterpoint exceeded 1,900 individual operations. In this respect, this program forms a considerable contrast to some of the codes to be discussed in connection with Experiment Three and Experiment Four, in which musical output of a less restricted nature was studied.

Experiment Three

Since the technical problems explored in this third section of work were rather varied, it is convenient to consider each separately and then describe how the various musical elements studied in this experiment were combined.

Rhythm. Rhythm was perhaps the most important musical element we felt had to be treated if a fundamental compositional technique utilizing computers was to be developed. Our objective in considering rhythm as a musical entity to be treated by computer processing was in accord with a recognition of this condition. It was our purpose to write a practical computer program for generating rhythms so that a fundamental technique might be demonstrated which in turn could form a basis for the further elaboration of rhythmic devices in more complex contexts.

Just as the notes of the scale can be represented by numbers in the computer, so also is it possible to symbolize rhythms numerically. In particular, the binary representation of numbers in the machine, consisting of permutations of ones and zeros, offered a convenient set of symbols with which we could operate. Thus, if we let 1 represent the "sounding," or "strike," of a note and 0 a "rest," or, alternatively, the "hold" of a previously sounded note, then we can let a sequence of ones and zeros represent a sequence of note values. For such sequences, ones and zeros, being integers, would each represent some arbitrarily chosen unit time interval, such as a quarter note, eighth note, or some smaller value. We next observe that a rhythmic pattern is generated by the interaction of these note values with meter, which is represented in turn by metrical patterns such as

$\frac{4}{4}, \frac{3}{4}, \frac{5}{8},$ or $\frac{6}{8}$. Thus, the production of a rhythmic structure not only involves the choice of note values, but also the choice between a repetitive or a varying meter and, moreover, the selection of which particular meter or meters to use. However, in order to keep the problem relatively simple in these first experiments, we arbitrarily restricted our studies to a simple metrical pattern, namely, $\frac{4}{8}$ meter, consisting of four eighth-notes to the measure. By further restricting the choice process to eighth notes as the smallest possible time intervals, we could then utilize simple permutations of four binary digits to represent the four beats of a measure in $\frac{4}{8}$ time. There are sixteen possible permutations of these four binary digits, permutations which also happen to represent the decimal numbers 0 through 15. These could be used to represent the possible rhythms in a $\frac{4}{8}$ measure, as shown in Table 11. Consequently, it was possible to propagate random integers between 0 and 15 and to let the values of these integers set the required rhythmic pattern for each measure. It might be noted at this point that rhythm in other metrical systems can also be generated by entirely similar processes. For triple meter, we generate random integers between 0 and 7, and for quintuple meter, random integers between 0 and 63.

Once the basic scheme for generating rhythms was set up, it was observed that, like note propagation, rhythm also is normally subjected to rules of composition and not permitted to occur entirely at random, except for the extreme case of random music, for which an appropriate random-integer table would have to be used. A table for this purpose would be based upon a scale of integers sufficiently extended so that the smallest useful time increment might be generated. It is to be noted that our rhythm-generation scheme, even though it can hardly be considered subject to much restriction, nevertheless represents a significant departure from this most extreme situation since no time intervals smaller than eighth notes were produced by it. Aside from this, however, if it were used as is, it would still generate a new rhythmic pattern in each voice in every measure produced. But rather than carry out this rather rudimentary process, it seemed desirable to proceed to something somewhat more challenging and to consider factors which might yield some rhythmic order over and above this relatively primitive situation. Since the simplest form of rhythmic redundancy is literal repetition, the first step we utilized to reduce further the randomness of the rhythm was a simple random repetition scheme. In each voice, a rhythmic pattern was generated according

Table 11
Basic Rhythmic Scheme for $\frac{4}{8}$ Meter

DECIMAL NUMBER	BINARY NUMBER	RHYTHMS CLOSED	OPEN
0	0000		
1	0001		
2	0010		
3	0011		
4	0100		
5	0101		
6	0110		
7	0111		
8	1000		
9	1001		
10	1010		
11	1011		
12	1100		
13	1101		
14	1110		
15	1111		

to the method outlined above and then a subsidiary random integer, which was permitted in our particular experiment to have values between 1 and 12, was also generated. This subsidiary parameter was used to control the number of measures a particular rhythmic pattern would be sustained before a new rhythmic pattern was generated for the voice in question. In this way, we obtained a variety of rhythmic patterns sustained for different lengths of time in the different voices. This was the first and simplest of the rhythm codes we produced.

It is a common characteristic of music, however, that there exist correlations of rhythms between the voices of a polyphonic piece of music. In the above rhythmic code, this does not happen except by pure coincidence. Therefore, the next step we considered was the introduction of some vertical as well as horizontal rhythmic redundancy. In a second rhythm code written for the Illiac, we included the generation of still a second subsidiary random integer, this random integer taking values from 0 through 15. In this code, use was made once again of binary notation as a type of musical symbolism. This time, in this new subsidiary random number, ones were used to represent voices required to play the same rhythm for the number of measures determined by the first subsidiary random integer, the lower voices being used as the master voices, while zeros were used to represent voices for which rhythms were generated independently. Thus, the representation 0000 meant that all voices would have independently generated rhythms, so that vertical duplications would occur only by coincidence. On the other hand, the representation 1111 was used to mean that all voices would have to play the same rhythm, the rhythm being that generated for the lowest voice. In between these two extremes, a representation such as 0101, for example, might be generated. This particular binary number indicated that Voices 2 and 4 would play the rhythm generated for Voice 2, while Voices 1 and 3 would be rhythmically free. It should be noted, however, that this redundancy scheme could not be rigidly applied because the integers 0001, 0010, 0100, and 1000 were meaningless in this application, i.e., these integers would have represented three voices free and one the same (as what?). Also, we could not represent the cases of two different pairs being the same separately, i.e., 1–2, 3–4; 1–3, 2–4; and 1–4, 2–3. Three of the above meaningless integers were therefore appropriated for these cases, leaving one integer which was disregarded. Lastly, the complication which arose the moment these two types of rhythmic redundancy were combined, namely, which would take precedence, was settled by letting the vertical-combinations rule take precedence.

The problem of notation of rhythm on the Teletype printout using ordinary symbols was handled by means of a makeshift code, utilizing a block of four digits to represent the rhythm in a given measure. We simply employed the binary number notation shown in Table 11 and printed twelve blocks, each consisting of four rows of four digits each, to represent the rhythm in twelve measures of four-part writing. An example of this will be illustrated in combination with other notation to be described.

This rhythm code was also arranged so that a new combination of rhythms would be generated at the beginning of each new line. There was no compelling reason for this; it was simply convenient to do so. This might also be regarded as one way of blocking in an extremely elementary longer-range structure for rhythmic patterns.

Dynamics. A second problem of considerable musical importance is the setting of dynamics. In Experiments One and Two, during the transcription of the experimental results to score form, an extremely simple scheme involving a four-integer random-integer table was employed to assign arbitrary dynamics marks to the individual voices (see Chapter 6). It was decided, however, to effect some improvement over this elementary technique, and not only place the generation of dynamics marks under the control of a computer program, but also include *crescendi and diminuendi* so that more than just terrace dynamics would occur.

This problem, in itself, is quite simple, and a set of operations similar to the rhythm scheme just described was worked out. The dynamic range was limited to *pp, p, mp, mf, f,* and *ff,* that is, to six possible values, so that the first operation became the simple process of generating a random integer considered equivalent to one of these dynamics marks. Secondly, a change of dynamics was indicated by means of a second random integer obtained from the possible choices 0, 1, or 2, which were considered equivalent to *diminuendo,* no change, and *crescendo.* In choosing this second random integer, restrictions had to be placed on the choice if *pp* or *ff,* the limits of the range, had been chosen previously, since *pp* could not be followed by *diminuendo,* and *ff* by *crescendo.* Therefore, a simple screening operation was inserted at this point to eliminate these two unacceptable possibilities.

Thirdly, the duration of the dynamics indication had to be set. Since this program was written in conjunction with the rhythm code just described, techniques similar to those used for the rhythm code were employed. In the simpler and earlier of the two codes actually written, a random integer which could take the values 0, 1, . . . , 12 was employed to set the dynamics scheme in each voice independently. In the second revised code, vertical correlation was used, just as in the rhythm code, so that all possible combinations from complete independence to complete agreement might be achieved.

The dynamics code was not correlated to the rhythm code. An entirely independent set of parameters governed the two operations, even though both were contained in the same computer program. Thus, the dynamic markings in Experiment Three are at no time correlated to rhythmic patterns or to changes in rhythm. Obviously, a correlation of one type or another could have been set up had we so desired, but for the sake of simplicity, this was not done.

Since letter notation is commonly employed to indicate dynamics, the printing of dynamic indications offered little difficulty. The letters F, P, and M were reserved for this purpose. To indicate *crescendo,* the symbol, (, was appropriated; to indicate constant dynamic level, the symbol, =, was used; while the symbol,), was used for *diminuendo.*

Orchestration Index. This is a name we have applied to the playing instructions which might be used to give color or timbre variation to the sound of the music being produced. In the most general sense, this can be thought of as the basis for a technique of instrumentation. In our experiments, since we planned the output for string quartet performance and thus had already made the choice of the particular instruments to be used, this problem resolved to the question of the various ways of playing stringed instruments. As is well known, there are numerous ways stringed instruments can be played, including various manners of bowing, several types of *pizzicato,* and a number of more sophisticated techniques, such as *col legno* (bowing with the wooden part of the bow), *sul ponticello* (playing on the bridge of the instrument), the playing of harmonics by causing the strings to vibrate in sections, and so on. In order to prepare a set of playing instructions, we selected sixteen of the most common stringed-instrument playing techniques and tabulated these as shown in Table 12. With the bowing instructions, we also included indications for transcription purposes as to whether a zero in the rhythmic code was to be observed as a sustained note or as a rest. These instructions for sustaining a note or for observing a rest were associated, as a general rule, with the bowing instructions with which they were most conveniently paired. Lastly, to allow for the fact that impossible combinations perform-

Table 12
Experiment Three
Orchestration Index

Random sexidecimal integer	Playing instructions	If playing instructions are impossible, revert to
0	Bowed *legato,* held through rests	F
1	Bowed *detaché,* rests observed	F
2	Bowed *tremolo,* hold through rests	0
3	Bowed *sul ponticello,* rests observed	1
4	Bowed, artificial harmonics, hold through rests	0
5	Bowed *col legno,* rests observed	1
6	Bowed *sul tasto,* hold through rests	0
7	Bowed *martellato,* rests observed	1
8	Bowed *legato* with mutes, hold through rests	0
9	Bowed, whole tone shake, rests observed	1
K	Bowed, *glissando* octave, hold through rests	0
S	Bowed ⌐· rests observed	1
N	Bowed ∨ rests observed	1
J	Snap *pizzicato*	F
F	Ordinary *pizzicato*	1
L	Rap on wooden body of instrument with knuckles	F

ancewise might arise if certain playing instructions were juxtaposed, we also permitted an alternative choice of simple *legato* or *pizzicato* to be used during transcription, just in case a playing instruction should turn out to be impossible. In actual fact, this was very seldom needed in transcribing this music for the *Illiac Suite.*

Once this list was prepared, it was possible to associate a numerical value with each instruction, and after so doing, we could use once again the technique previously employed to establish rhythm and dynamics indications. Thus, it was possible to generate random integers between the values 0, 1, . . . , 15 in order to indicate particular playing instructions for the various instruments. Moreover, as in the cases of rhythm and dynamics, it was also possible to establish how long and to which instruments each playing instruction was to be assigned. Consequently, the same two schemes for horizontal and vertical organization were incorporated into this code as had been used for the rhythm code. In the earlier experiments, a playing instruction was assigned to each instrument independently for any random length up to twelve measures, after which time a new playing instruction was generated for the voice in question. In the revised code, as with the rhythm instructions, simple vertical redundancy was introduced to tie the four voices together a little more closely.

Combination of Rhythm, Dynamics, and Playing Instructions. We have already explained how the representation of rhythm on the Teletype printout was planned. In actual fact, instructions for controlling all three of the above-described musical elements were written as one single computer program so that rhythm, dynamics, and playing instructions were produced successively. The printout for all three was arranged in the most compact form for legibility, with the dynamics and playing instructions for each voice being placed immediately under the rhythmic indication for the same voice. An example of actual computer output produced by the more basic of these two programs for these musical elements is shown in Figure 9,

0101	0101	0101	0101	0101	0101
6 FF=	6 FF=	6 FF=	6 FF=	6 FF=	6 FF=
0111	0111	0111	0111	0111	0111
S PP(	S MF(	S MF(	L MF(	7 MF(	L MF(
1010	1010	1010	1010	1010	1010
9 FF)	9 FF)	9 FF)	N F=	N F=	5 F=
1101	1101	1101	0111	0111	0111
J F)	8 F)	8 F)	8 P(	8 P(	8 P(

Figure 9. Experiment Three: Sample of computer output from the simplest program for rhythm, dynamics, and playing instructions.

while in Figure 10, the transcription of these same results into score form is shown.

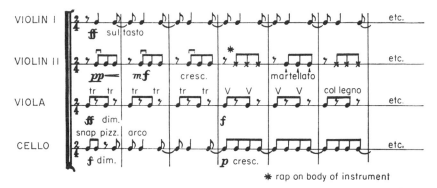

Figure 10. Experiment Three: Transcription of the computer output shown in Figure 9.

Random Chromatic Music. The music shown in Figure 10 lacks any indication of pitch; thus, the next logical step was to develop a program for note selection which would differ from what was done previously with strict counterpoint. For reasons already discussed, we decided to set up a freer basis for note selection and to establish a minimum technique for music writing which would be closer to contemporary practices than strict counterpoint. The first step was to renumber the notes of the scale to include all chromatic steps, black as well as white notes in terms of the piano keyboard. Therefore, for a basic chromatic scale, we used the integers 0–30, which were considered to correspond to a range of two and one-half octaves from C to F#″, C being interpreted as the lowest playable C for each of the four instruments. Starting the range of notes with C was convenient, since both the viola and cello have this as their lowest note. The actual process of generating random music involving these thirty-one notes was, of course, extremely simple and involved no more than random-integer generation with the multiplier 31, utilizing the process already described in Chapter 4. At the same time, an improved printout program was written to print the selected notes in letter rather than number notation. In adapting the conventional Teletype machine to this purpose, the letters A through G were used to indicate the notes themselves, the letter X to indicate sharpened notes (F sharp being printed as FX, for example), and primes to indicate the first and second octaves above the lowest octave. For the sake of simplicity, notation for flattened notes was eliminated. The printing of the results was matched to the rhythm code described above, so that the notes and rhythms lined up in a simple four-to-one correspondence. Thus, one line of notes became the equivalent of three measures of rhythm. Actually, the two basic programs, the one for rhythm and allied musical elements and the other for note selection, were kept separate. This was done simply for convenience, so that each could be revised and made more complex independently and with a minimum amount of rewriting.

Simple Chromatic Music. It was of interest to carry out at least one experiment with random chromatic music to illustrate how a degree of order might be imposed upon this elementary material by simple means. Therefore, in order to write a second type of chromatic music, four compositional rules were imposed on the selection process. The particular rules selected for this purpose were employed because it was felt that these rules would impose a relatively high degree of order with a minimum of actual instructions. The following rules were coded for the Illiac.

Rule 1. This was the melodic skip-stepwise rule already familiar in the strict counterpoint code. This rule was used substantially unchanged except for adjustments required in going from white-note to chromatic music. In the present application, we permitted only melodic movements of a whole tone or less—i.e., a whole tone or a half tone in either direction or a repeated note—to follow a melodic motion greater than a whole tone. On the other hand, any melodic movement obeying the rules in general was permitted to follow a stepwise melodic movement of a whole tone or less.

Rule 2. This was a melodic octave-range rule, also adapted from strict counterpoint. The octave range was set to apply as far back as twenty-four notes, i.e., six measures, maximum. After every three measures, corresponding to one line of printout, had been completed, however, the backward extent of scanning for the octave range was moved up three measures, thus permitting the octave range to be changed in accord with the contents of the last three measures only. This procedure permitted the formation of a new octave range whenever these three last measures contained a melodic substance spanning less than an octave. This octave-range rule, moreover, was affected by the tritone-resolution process to be discussed immediately below.

Rule 3. A rather complex way of resolving tritones was set up which provided the only harmonic control over the musical material being generated. The rule is a simple example of how a reasonable compositional rule can be devised for computer use which helps set up an appropriate control process in a special situation.

Tritones can occur between the four voices in the following ways:

1. A single tritone (only two voices involved)
2. Two independent tritones (all four voices involved)
3. A single tritone with one repeated note (three voices involved)
4. A single tritone with a single note repeated twice (all four voices involved)
5. A single tritone with both notes repeated once (all four voices involved)

(Notes differing by a multiple of an octave were considered equivalent for the purpose of this tritone-resolution rule.)

In the case of the tritones involving no repeated notes, specifically, Cases 1 and 2, the resolution was required to take place by contrary half-tone steps either inwards or outwards, depending upon the result of a binary random choice. For Case 3, the resolution between the single note and one of the two repeated notes was required to be the same as the above, but the other repeated note was permitted to resolve contrary to the first repeated note by a stepwise movement of zero to four half-tones chosen at random. Case 4 was resolved the same way as Case 3, except the fourth voice was permitted to move freely. Finally, Case 5 was resolved by requiring two stepwise motions and two motions of zero to four half-tones chosen at random but in contrary motion to the stepwise movements.

Rule 4. As a last rule, whenever the octave-range rule was violated by a tritone resolution, the resolution was permitted, and the reference point for the octave range was moved up timewise in the musical structure so that the rule would again be satisfied; that is to say, a new octave range was set by the tritone-resolution note. It should be noted that this fourth rule is of considerable interest because it is a simple example of a built-in rule-revision process. The applicable octave range was generated during the course of the first three measures of a given melodic line. It then restricted the range of the melody in accord with Rule 2 until a tritone resolution occurred to force the computer to erase the octave-range limitation in effect and set up a new octave range which had as one of its limits the note farthest back in the melody which was an octave or less separated from the note of the tritone resolution which brought about the revision of the octave range. The operation of this process is shown in Figure 11.

In the computer, the tritone type could be determined after each chord was generated by counting how many times the four voices entered into tritones and then summing. This summing process is illustrated in Table 13. Only in Cases 2 and 3 was there any ambiguity resulting from this

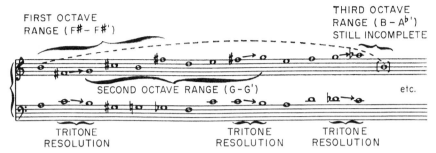

Figure 11. Experiment Three: Illustration of how the octave-range rule is revised by tritone resolutions.

summation process, but this could be resolved by noting that one of the counters was zero in Case 3.

The actual computing process for the application of these compositional rules is shown in condensed form as the block diagram in Figure 12. It is seen that the same general logical outline was required as that used for the strict counterpoint routine previously discussed, and that the initial step in planning the actual program for the Illiac was to decide upon an efficient way of organizing the rules. After the initial entry, which, as in earlier codes, involved the various routine operations required to get the calculations started, the computation cycle was immediately entered at the point at which tritone resolutions were carried out and the test for skip-stepwise motion was made. Naturally, for the first chord, these rules were bypassed, and a random note immediately generated for the first voice and later, upon recycling, for the other three voices as well.

In general, the tritone-resolution operation was divided into three basic operations. Further along in the process, it is observed that the new note in each voice was tested for whether it had occurred in a vertical tritone

Table 13
Experiment Three
Detection of Tritone Combinations by Counting the Number
of Voices in Tritone Combination

Tritone type		V_1	V_2	V_3	V_4	ΣV_i
Case 1	1100	1	1	0	0	2
Case 2	1111	1	1	1	1	4
Case 3	2110	2	1	1	0	4
Case 4	3111	3	1	1	1	6
Case 5	2222	2	2	2	2	8

relationship with any other voices already generated. If not, then the recycling operation was carried out, unless it was the fourth voice being produced, in which case the next part of the program was entered.

On the other hand, if a tritone was found, then a record was made of the voices between which the interval occurred. This was done by adding unit increments into assigned storage locations in the computer. Four spaces in the computer memory were reserved for Voices 1 to 4, respectively, as counting locations for tritone intervals. Two counters were stepped up by one unit each by this operation, as shown in the block entitled "Step two counters" in Figure 12. An example of how this works is shown in Table 14.

After the counting of all the tritones was completed, the second part of the tritone-resolution process was carried out. This was the summation operation already shown in Table 13. The counters in the four locations were simply summed. If the sum ΣV_i was found to be zero, then we knew

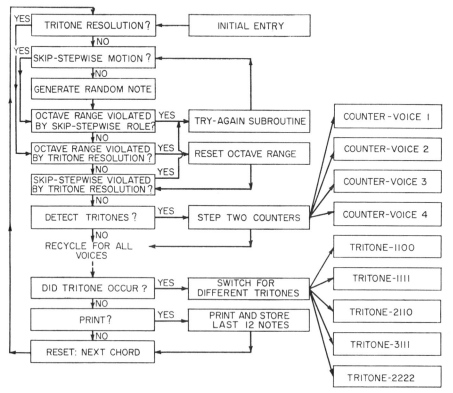

Figure 12. Experiment Three: Block diagram for chromatic writing.

Table 14
Experiment Three
An Example of the Operation of the Tritone Counter

	Storage locations			
	Voice 1	Voice 2	Voice 3	Voice 4
Initially	0	0	0	0
Tritone detected between Voices 1 and 3, add	+1	0	+1	0
Result in counter	+1	0	+1	0
Tritone detected between Voices 1 and 4, add	+1	0	0	+1
Result	+2	0	+1	+1

that no tritone had occurred. A bypass of the actual tritone-resolution process was then inserted by placing an unconditional transfer order to the skip-stepwise motion test in front of this resolution operation. On the other hand, if this sum was found to be unequal to zero, an unconditional transfer direct to the tritone-resolution routine was inserted immediately before the routine. The particular tritone case was then detected by determining the magnitude of the sum ΣV_i. This was done by a simple additive technique of the type already discussed in the descriptions of Experiments One and Two. In addition, it should be noted that the counters gave a record also of which particular voices were involved. This was essential information, since a simple tritone of the form 1100, for example, can exist in a number of permutations, such as 1100, 1010, 1001, 0110, 0101, and 0011, considering the four digits to represent Voices 1 to 4, respectively, in that order.

After detecting the tritone type by means of the sum ΣV_i, and after a small extra test in case this sum was found equal to 4, a switch was employed to direct the operations to the particular type of tritone resolution required in accord with the rules given earlier. Cases 1 and 2 could be treated by the same basic routine, Case 2 simply involving a repeat of the operation, the operation itself being a simple random binary choice to determine whether the resolution would be inwards or outwards, followed by the actual recording of the required new notes. Cases 3 and 4 could also be treated essentially as a pair, since in Case 4, the fourth voice was allowed to move freely. In these cases, a random choice was first made of which of the doubled voices would be required to move stepwise. Then,

a second random choice, this time a binary choice, was made to determine
the direction of the resolution. In Case 3, the remaining voice was then
required to move by contrary motion in accord with the rule described
above, while in Case 4, a further choice had to be made, namely, to decide
which of the remaining doubled voices would be required to move stepwise
and which would be permitted to move freely. Case 5, lastly, was a bit
more complex. Two random binary choices were first generated in order
to determine which voice in each of the two doubled pairs involved in the
tritone interval would be selected for stepwise resolution. Then, another
binary random choice was generated to determine whether the resolution
would occur inwards or outwards. Finally, the remaining voices were required to move in contrary motion to their doubled partners and, hence,
in respect to one another. In all five cases, the contrary-motion process
made use of a simple five-choice random-integer-choice operation followed
by the selection of the correct sign for contrary motion.

Between the test for tritones and the actual carrying out of the tritone
resolutions if tritones were found, it was necessary to insert two other
operations. As shown in Figure 12, the first of these was a set of printing
instructions which was activated by a counter after every twelve chords
had been formed. This operation caused the computer to punch tape which
would result in one line of printed output. Simultaneously, this completed
line of output was stored in the computer memory, overwriting the previous line of output, so that the octave-range rule could be applied backwards for three measures beyond the new line to be compared. In addition, independently of these printing instructions, counters and various
other routines were set so that the next chord would be generated.

The operation of the remaining sets of instructions is rather obvious in
the light of the detailed descriptions given of similar rules applied in Experiments One and Two. The skip-stepwise-motion routine was set up
entirely similarly to the related strict counterpoint rule, with the necessary
modifications required to permit chromatic motion. The octave-range rule
likewise was adapted from the operations used for the strict counterpoint
program. The resetting of the octave-range by the tritone-resolution process
was extremely simple and involved merely the resetting of two storage
indices used for this computation. Lastly, the try-again subroutine was the
same as that used before, except for minor bookkeeping details.

Interval and Tone Rows. One simple way to initiate a study of the relationship between entropy and melody is to consider a twelve-note melody.
If we were to tabulate all possible twelve-note melodies, we would see that

the number of possible melodies could be expressed in terms of elementary permutation theory. Thus, if we require only that the twelve notes be selected from twelve possible tones with no restrictions in regard to repeats of tones being required or forbidden, we observe that we have defined the condition of random music within this limited situation. If this condition applies to all twelve notes, 12^{12} melodies are theoretically possible —an enormously large number. This is a situation of maximum entropy, or information, content in terms of the choice process, but it is not necessarily the condition of maximum entropy content in terms of tonality. This can be arrived at by a somewhat different procedure. Let us first note that among all types of melodies in this random situation, the variety of melodic types extends from the case in which all twelve tones of the melodies are required to be the same to the case in which all twelve tones are required to be different. At one end of this spectrum, where all the tones are required to be the same, there exists a minimum of entropy— i.e., a maximum of redundancy—because the total possible number of melodies is just twelve if we permit full freedom of choice for the first tone and just one if we restrict this choice to one specific pitch. This is obviously totally established tonality—twelve repeats of the same tone. At the other end of the spectrum, however, where the twelve tones are all required to be different, each tone of the chromatic scale is sounded just once in some specific order which may or may not be randomly produced. This is, of course, the tone-row concept first significantly exploited by Arnold Schönberg. The fact that the specification of a tone row is arrived at by precisely the opposite technique as that of "ultimate tonality," namely, by requiring that the tones be different as contrasted to requiring them to be the same, suggests the thought that a tone row is not just simply an atonal device, but rather that it is a specific "antitonal" construction which, within its own length, is deliberately devised to exclude the type of redundancy required to set up tonality. Atonality, as a term, is therefore better applied to the situation of random music rather than to constructions such as tone rows. In this way, tone rows present rather interesting musical properties, since they represent not only a highly restrictive and easily managed technique for reducing the entropy content of random music, but also an extreme condition in terms of elementary permutation theory and a computational extreme for counteracting conventional tonality. It can be readily shown that the total number of possible tone rows is 12!,[4] which, although it is a relatively large number, is considerably less

[4] $12! = 12 \cdot 11 \cdot 10 \cdot 9 \cdot 8 \cdot 7 \cdot 6 \cdot 5 \cdot 4 \cdot 3 \cdot 2 \cdot 1 = 479,001,600.$

than the total possible number of twelve-note melodies. Moreover, in everyday practice, the total possible number of such melodies is effectively much less than this, since one type of redundancy commonly employed in tone-row compositions is that based upon permutation techniques such as inversion, retrogression, and the like. It is important to note also that transposition, of course, does not alter the basic character of tone rows any more than it does other types of melodic lines. This is equivalent to saying that there are really only 11! rather than 12! possible tone rows, since the particular pitch level at which the row is played is of secondary consequence compared to the actual profile of the row. In view of what we said earlier in Chapter 2, we may then infer that the melodic profile of a tone row depends *not upon a succession of the twelve tones of the chromatic scale* as such, as is often commonly supposed, but upon the *mutual interrelationships between the twelve notes in terms of intervals.* Since in theory at least all the twelve tones are presumed to be of equivalent importance, the melodic profile is, therefore, a series of intervals between successive notes in which any one or all of the twelve notes can be selected as a reference point. Once a reference point is defined, it is observed that the tone row consists actually of a series of all the possible melodic intervals considered not in succession but in relation to this reference tone. To make this point clear, we may arbitrarily choose the first note of a tone row as the reference tone and then illustrate by an example. In Figure 13, a typical tone row is

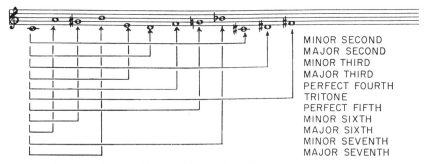

Figure 13. Experiment Three: Illustration of how all the possible intervals occur in a row of twelve different tones.

shown. It contains all the possible melodic intervals from a minor second to a major seventh *in relation to the first note of the row,* C (or, for that matter, in relation to any other note of the row). Moreover, each one of the intervals, which we may define now as the difference $N_i - N_1$, using the notation adopted previously for notes and intervals, occurs *once and only once,* but the intervals found between successive tones $N_i - N_{i-1}$, $N_{i+1} - N_i$, etc., may occur more than once. Thus, repeats of *successive* melodic intervals are not forbidden.

On the other hand, we can also write rows in which repeats of successive melodic intervals of the type $N_i - N_{i-1}$ are forbidden, but repeats of reference intervals of the type $N_i - N_1$ are permitted. This produces what we can call an *interval row* as opposed to a tone row. The interval row perhaps is a new type of melodic structure, which should present some interesting musical properties, particularly in light of the experiments to be described under Experiment Four, in which the properties of different varieties of melodic intervals, both successive and long range, are examined in greater detail.[4a] A typical interval row is shown in Figure 14. It should

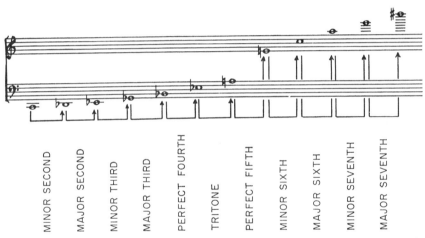

Figure 14. Experiment Three: A typical interval row, not showing transpositions to reduce span of row.

be noted that actual tones or their octave equivalents can be repeated in an interval row in contrast to the tone row. It is not necessarily a situation of greater redundancy than that of tone rows, however, since both permit the same total number of possible choices. Redundancy in terms of tonality is greater in the case of interval rows, but whether this is, in terms of musical meaning, a situation of greater redundancy depends on whether successive or referential intervals are to be considered the more significant in the con-

[4a] It might be noted parenthetically that since working on this computer music, one of the present authors (L. A. H.) has written an extended piano composition based in part on this notion of an interval row.

struction of melodies. In any event, we may note that both tone rows and interval rows have similar specific constraints imposed upon them in regard to repetition of choices. In both choice processes, eleven choices of intervals are permitted initially, but each time an interval is chosen, it is excluded from the remaining choices to be made. This is analogous to the problem of choosing colored balls from a box and *not replacing them after each choice,* as opposed to a random succession which occurs when the balls are replaced. It is by analysis of this process that the value of 11! is arrived at. Within this particular choice process, we may also observe that the difference between a tone row and an interval row is the following: A tone row is an *i*th-order Markoff process, while an interval row is a zeroth-order Markoff process in terms of how the intervals are evaluated. This difference is made clear if the reference states in Figures 13 and 14 are compared.

Once we agree to the foregoing analysis of the properties of interval rows and tone rows, it becomes simple to write a program for the computer for generating these types of musical structures, of which the tone row, at least, is at the present time a frequently used compositional device. The concluding part of Experiment Three, therefore, consisted of three related programs for the Illiac for generating (1) interval rows of the type described above, (2) tone rows, also of the type described above, and (3) tone rows of a somewhat more restricted character. These last tone rows were written at the suggestion of Robert Kelly, of the School of Music at the University of Illinois, and are rather freely based upon a pedagogical approach to music writing developed by this author for teaching counterpoint and harmony from a contemporary viewpoint in beginning composition courses.[5] The method combines certain properties of tone rows with adaptations of a number of the rules of strict counterpoint. The rules employed by Kelly are given in the cited reference. Our adjustments of these rules for computer processing are the following:

Rule 1. The theme should consist of thirteen notes using all twelve tones, with the first and last notes being C.

Rule 2. A span of a major tenth is set as the limit for the melodic range.

Rule 3. Progressions of major sevenths, minor sevenths, and tritones are forbidden.

Rule 4. No tied-over notes are permitted. This rule was automatically taken care of the way the tone-row generation scheme was set up (see below).

---

[5] R. Kelly, *Theme and Variations, A Study of Linear Twelve-tone Composition,* Wm. C. Brown Co., Dubuque, Iowa, 1958. pp. 2–4.

Rule 5. Chromatic progressions in the same direction involving three or more consecutive notes are forbidden.

Rule 6. The skip-stepwise rule is modified to permit two skips in the same direction.

Rule 7. Consecutive sets of three notes that constitute a triad may occur at random.

Rule 8. No tritone is permitted for $N_i - N_{i-1}$ unless $N_{i-1} - N_{i-2} = \pm 1$, or, alternatively, 5 or 7 in the same direction as the tritone.

Rule 9. The use of sequences is prohibited. In other words, $N_i - N_{i-1}$ cannot equal $N_{i-2} - N_{i-3}$, and so on.

It can be seen immediately that a block diagram for a testing procedure similar to those shown already for Experiments Two and Three could be designed, and from this a testing program written which would include the usual type of try-again subroutine. This testing procedure was written as a subroutine which was grafted onto the basic interval and tone-row-generation program described below. Since this subroutine involved no basically different programming techniques from those already described, it seems unnecessary to consider its details, since these largely duplicate what we have already discussed.

The Generation of Interval and Tone Rows. The production of interval and tone rows was quite simple to carry out in the Illiac. The main routine for this process was designed as follows: To make the note-selection process efficient, a small table containing numerical representations from one to twelve was stored in the computer. These were considered to be numerical representations for all the possible intervals from a minor second to an octave which simultaneously gave a count for each interval of the number of half-tone steps within the interval. The unison or repeat (numerical representation = 0) was omitted from this table, since it was decided to apply Kelly's procedure of writing *cantus firmi* of thirteen notes, of which the first and, in the tone rows, the last would be set automatically as C. An interval was then selected at random from the above-described interval table and *added* to the interval or tone-row representation being formed to obtain the first *tone* in the sequence of the interval or tone row. This interval was then removed from the table, and all entries below it were moved up one line and the process repeated. Thus, we started with twelve possible choices, then went successively to eleven choices, ten choices, and so on, until we were left with only one choice for the final interval. When an interval or tone row was completed, it was then printed out and the computer reset to perform the operation all over again.

The way in which the intervals being selected at random were added to the row being formed determined whether or not an interval or tone row was formed. In view of our earlier discussion, the difference is seen to be one of minor coding changes. To produce an interval row, the numerical representation of the interval just chosen was added to the previous note in the row to produce a new note in the row separated from the previous note by the interval in question. However, since we always *added* new intervals to a row to give upward progressions, it became necessary to employ also an octave-subtraction process, because otherwise the span of the row would soon exceed the set limit of two and one-half octaves of the chromatic scale. This is in accord with normal practice, however, for subtracting an octave from a note does not disturb its primary functional relationship to a melodic reference point such as the first note of the melodic line. What we actually did in the generation of interval rows was to make a binary choice which determined whether we would simply *add* the interval to the previous note and, therefore, move upwards in pitch or, alternatively, *add* the note and then *subtract* one octave to produce a note lower than the last. Secondly, it was also necessary to test for whether the limits of the chromatic scale being used were being exceeded in spite of this. Therefore, a test was also made to determine whether this was so, and if necessary, and adjustment of the movement in the proper direction, either upwards or downwards, as the case might be, was then made. Finally, it was observed that an interval row starting on C always of necessity ends on F sharp.

To produce tone rows rather then interval rows, the interval randomly selected from the table was simply added to the *first note* C of the row, rather than to the previous note in the row. This automatically produced a tone row rather than an interval row. Otherwise, the whole process was kept exactly the same, except that the octave was removed from the table of intervals, since the choice of this interval would lead to the repeat of a *tone* (or its octave equivalent) within a tone row. This would be a violation of the requirements for such a row. In generating simple tone rows of thirteen notes according to the chosen plan but with no restrictions, we simply arbitrarily made this the *last* interval to be selected, so that the row this time would of necessity have C or its octave equivalent as its final note. In the case of the restricted tone rows, in addition to writing a subroutine which would apply the rules given above, we could simply eliminate the octave from consideration as a possible interval.

Tone-row Permutations. A basic procedure in writing tone-row music is to perform geometrical permutations upon the row being utilized to compose a piece of music. There are many possible geometrical operations upon tone rows which can be used, but of these the three simplest and most frequently used are inversion, i.e., writing each interval downwards instead of upwards, retrogression, i.e., writing the row backwards, and lastly, inversion of the retrograde form of the row.[6, 7] In the computer, these geometrical permutations were most easily carried out as part of the printout procedure. In this way, they are handled rather analogously to the process of transposition which we shall consider under Experiment Four. We arranged the printout to contain in a block of four lines: (1) the row itself, (2) its inversion, (3) the retrograde form, and (4) the retrograde inversion, each printed one under the other. The printing of these four forms of a row was just a matter of format arrangement for the printout routine. The row itself was first printed a symbol at a time, each numerical representation of a note being converted into its letter equivalent. Secondly, the inversion of the row was formed by changing the signs of the successive intervals in the row and then printing out the letter equivalents of the notes of the inverted row. Lastly, the two retrograde forms were produced by printing out these two forms of the row again, but selecting the notes in reverse order.

Experiment Four

The objectives of Experiment Four differed from those of previous experiments, since it was our purpose in this new experiment to generate samples of music based upon certain more abstract formulations which we believed might eventually be related to structural devices in musical composition such as tonality and melodic profile. In the first three experiments,

[6] Strictly speaking, one should differentiate between retrograde inversions and inverted retrograde rows, since these two variations, although they have the same profile, may not occur at the same pitch, depending upon the last note in a row. Thus, a tone row beginning on C and ending on E, for example, will have a retrograde inversion beginning on A flat and ending on C, while the inverted retrograde form of the row will start on E and end on G sharp. The recognition of this difference, of course, produces a modulatory technique in tone-row writing. In our samples, however, which begin and end on C, this problem did not arise because of symmetry considerations. This also happens to be true for the interval rows as well, since these must of necessity end on F sharp, which is likewise a situation of symmetry.

[7] It is perhaps also desirable to note, in passing, that these basic techniques are, of course, by no means unique to row writing. As is well known to musicians, all these, as well as many other geometrical operations, are common procedures in many types of well-established musical forms such as, for example, in canons and fugues.

and particularly the first two, we were primarily concerned with the generation of music recognizable in many respects as falling within the traditional
framework of compositional procedures. In Experiment Four, this was no
longer intended to be the case. In this last set of experiments, simpler and
perhaps more fundamental means of musical construction were investigated
than those studied previously. This was done in an attempt to find more
inclusive concepts to work with, and, in particular, concepts which might be
thought of as geometrical analogs of musical form.

The fundamental geometrical picture selected was an abstraction of the
calculating technique used in the three previous experiments. The generation of four-part musical structures was pictured as a restricted random-
flight problem in which four trajectories are traced simultaneously upon the
rather unusual coordinate system of pitch versus time. This geometrical
structure, illustrated in Figure 15, can be subjected to mathematical defini-

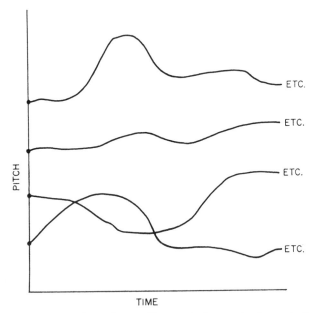

Figure 15. Experiment Four: A four-voiced musical
texture pictured as a random-flight problem.

tion, as we have already indicated in Chapters 2, 3, and 4. It is particularly
characterized in terms of Markoff chain processes, i.e., sequences of events
in which the choice of each new event can be made dependent upon pre-

vious events; or, in musical terms, the choice of each new note or interval in a given melodic line can be made dependent upon previous notes or intervals in the same melodic line. Utilizing this simple picture, we wrote computer programs for generating a series of samples of what we may call *Markoff chain music*.

Harmonic and Proximity Functions in Melodic Construction. If we recall the dependences of melodic construction and tonality upon both the successive and long-range intervallic relationships discussed in Chapter 2, we may now note that successive melodic intervals bear three significant characteristics which *may* be used to impart formal structure to a melody: (1) Melodic intervals can be related to the overtone series so that we recognize a harmonic function in melodic construction. Thus, the outlining of a triad, C–E–G for example, imparts a sense of C major, or, at least, of the C–major chord, and a sense of relatively high tonal order. On the other hand, a sequence such as F–A flat–D is more ambiguous and conveys a number of possible implications in terms of structural function, other factors being equal. (2) Melodic intervals may also be characterized by their absolute size. Thus, stepwise melodic progressions such as half-tone or whole-tone intervals seem to impart more order than larger skips such as sevenths, octaves, and larger intervals. (3) We may note that many well-constructed melodies consist of sequences of intervals which balance the tendencies to order and disorder by balancing harmonic clarity with ambiguity, and stepwise melodic movements with larger skips. Even in music in which these principles seem to operate minimally, as in certain types of contemporary music, the presence of both functions, which we may now call *harmonic* and *proximity* functions, can be traced. In a way, this can be said to be true even indirectly of the steps resorted to by composers in negating tonality by devices such as twelve-tone rows.

Relation to Musical Structure. These two functions can also be examined somewhat more broadly than just in terms of relatively short-range melodic relationships. In terms of more recent musical styles, these two functions of harmonic and intervallic structure also form the basis of many of the more searching analyses of musical forms such as, to cite two representative and well-known authors, those by Hindemith[8] and by Schenker,[9] whose

[8] P. Hindemith, *Craft of Musical Composition—I. Theory*, rev. ed. (trans. by A. Mendel), Associated Music Publishers, Inc., New York, 1945.

[9] H. Schenker, *Neue Musikalische Theorien und Phantasien:* vol. I, *Harmonielehre,* 1906, vol. II, *Contrapunkt,* 1910 and 1920, vol. III, *Die Freie Satz,* 1935. Universal Edition, Vienna.

concepts have been presented in English by Katz,[10] Salzer,[11] and Jonas and Borgese.[12]

Both Hindemith and Schenker distinguish the harmonic and melodic element, and both acknowledge the dependence of the harmonic elements upon recognizable relationships to the harmonic series and of the melodic element upon stepwise motions. Thus, Hindemith stresses the importance of "root-progressions," of which the strongest harmonically are shifts, such as fifths, fourths, and thirds, in giving convincing harmonic movement to musical passages.[13] He also remarks that a smooth and convincing melodic outline is achieved only when these important points form progressions in seconds.[14]

However, Hindemith confines himself almost wholly to successive musical relationships, leaving the question of larger structures relatively unexplored; therefore, we might also consider Schenker's ideas, which are somewhat more ambitious in scope. He suggested that elements of a musical structure could be compared to a series of structural layers, starting from a "foreground" which is the complete work as we hear it to a "background" structure in which only a skeletal framework of the music is left. In analyzing a piece of music, Schenker proposed that these layers can be successively stripped away to reveal the basic framework, which he called the *ursatz* and which he thought consisted of two basic elements. The first we can interpret as the essential harmonic root movement of a whole structural unit, such as a song or sonata-allegro form. He postulated that all satisfactory musical forms, even lengthy ones, could be simplified to one of several simple root progressions, such as I–III–V–I and I–IV–V–I, and was able to build quite a good argument for this idea by utilizing exclusively examples from the works of the master composers of the eighteenth and nineteenth centuries, the only repertory he considered admissible. The second element of the *ursatz* proposed by Schenker is the *urlinie*. This is a significant essential descending melodic line contained in every "acceptable" piece of music. The *urlinie* is always basically simple, being a sequence such as, in C, G–F–E–D–C. Complex musical structures are then built up by elaboration upon these two elements of the simple skeletal

[10] A. Katz, *Challenge to Musical Tradition,* Alfred A. Knopf, Inc., New York, 1945.

[11] F. Salzer, *Structural Hearing; Tonal Coherence in Music,* Albert and Charles Boni, Inc., New York, 1952.

[12] H. Schenker, *Harmony,* from *Harmonielehre,* ref. 9 above (ed. by O. Jonas and trans. by E. M. Borgese), University of Chicago Press, Chicago, 1954.

[13] Hindemith, *op. cit.,* chap. IV in particular.

[14] *Ibid.,* p. 193.

framework. The principles of the theory are supposed to be in operation within sections of a piece of music in a subsidiary role as well as over the whole musical structure. Many examples of how the Schenker system of analysis can be applied are given in Salzer's book; it is to be noted that Salzer goes to considerable effort to circumvent Schenker's dogmatic attitudes regarding the absolute superiority of Germanic music from 1700 to 1900, which has marred the impression of his work in the eyes of some critics.[15] It is not our purpose to become involved in detailed criticisms of methods of musical analysis, but only to extract from them several ideas which were useful in planning the experiments to be described and which would be of paramount importance in any future experiments in which more elaborate musical structure might be produced. The first is the concept of structural frameworks, both harmonic and melodic. This concept is useful because it provides a differentiation between structural points of greater or lesser significance. A working technique for structural assembly is thus provided that permits the assigning of a greater or lesser value to significant musical elements, particularly in relation to the time scale of the musical structure. It is observed that this factor is almost entirely missing in the computer music produced in the first three experiments.

The second basic point is the emphasis on a distinct harmonic element and a distinct melodic element in the basic structure. This does seem to be in general accord with our definitions of a harmonic and a proximity function, and suggests a method of elaboration of the techniques shortly to be described under Experiment Four for the construction of more complex musical structures. The particular emphasis by analysts such as Schenker on the practices of the eighteenth and nineteenth centuries, which established for them a standard for clarity of tonality, need not be mistaken for an absolute necessity. If we consider musical structures antecedent to 1700 as a source of ideas, we can observe that this music was written before the concept of tonality was clearly defined. Thus, in view of the emphasis on contrapuntal rules rather than harmony in this earlier music, the proximity-type function might be found to play a more preponderant role here. Moreover, closeness of intervals seems to have been used as a guiding principle, not only for simple step-by-step techniques, such as the skip-stepwise rule of counterpoint, but also implicitly as an important structural device in,

[15] M. Mann, "Schenker's Contribution to Music Theory," *Music Review*, 10:3–26, 1949; R. Sessions, "Heinrich Schenker's Contribution," *Modern Music*, 12:170–178, 1935; R. Sessions, "Escape by Theory," *Modern Music*, 15:192–197, 1938. This last article in particular is a highly critical review of Schenker's *Die Freie Satz*.

for example, much primitive music, non-Western music, and in older Western art music such as plain chant. Coherence is not infrequently brought about by melismatic weaving about certain structurally important melodic notes, or even around one fixed tonal center. This might also be true in certain types of contemporary music as well. Thus, Hindemith,[8] for example, permits in his system of composition a structural dependence on proximity, or neighbor-note relationships, as well as on strongly harmonic relationships such as the fifth, fourth, and third.

Table of Weighted Probabilities. In order to institute an analytical study of these processes, we first defined a harmonic function x_j and a proximity function y_j. Then, to investigate how these functions might operate to produce melodic structures, a series of experiments was carried out in which Markoff chain processes were used as a basic computing technique. The first requirement was a reference table of weighted transition probabilities stored in the computer, to be utilized as required. It should be noted that, in essence, this had been done all along in previous experiments, but in these earlier experiments, the transition probabilities were usually either simple random-choice situations, i.e., all choices were weighted equally, or else some of the choices were simply forbidden and thus given zero weight. The counterpoint rules, for example, often amount to no more than just this. The second requirement we imposed was that this table must contain as few bits of basic information as possible, but that this information be of as fundamental significance as possible. In this way, we hoped to investigate how to avoid the problem of high-capacity information storage, which currently presents such a major difficulty in many other data-processing problems such as language translation by machine. Therefore, a table was constructed for arranging all successive melodic intervals from the unison (melodically, the repeat) to the octave. This is shown in Table 15, where the various possible melodic intervals are listed first in descending order of consonance from the repeat to the tritone. For the purpose of machine calculations, we associated with each interval a value of a stochastic variable v_j, which runs from 0 for the unison, or repeat, to 12 for the octave. These are the values we could add or subtract to each *tone* of a melody to obtain the next *tone* of the melody, which resulted as a consequence of moving through the interval represented by the variable. A melody could, therefore, be symbolized by a sequence of values $v_i = v_1, v_2, \ldots, v_n$, added successively to the first note of the melody. In the present work, the note C was normally selected as an arbitrary starting point. Once again, as in previous studies such as that of interval and tone rows, intervals,

Table 15
Table of Functions for the Generation of
Markoff Chain Music in Experiment Four

Interval	Stochastic variable v_j	Harmonic function x_j	Proximity function y_j	Combined function $z_j = x_j + y_j$
Unison	0	13	13	26
Octave	12	12	1	13
Fifth	7	11	6	17
Fourth	5	10	8	18
Major third	4	9	9	18
Minor sixth	8	8	5	13
Minor third	3	7	10	17
Major sixth	9	6	4	10
Major second	2	5	11	16
Minor seventh	10	4	3	7
Minor second	1	3	12	15
Major seventh	11	2	2	4
Tritone	6	1	7	8

$$\sum_{j=0}^{12} x_j = 91 \qquad \sum_{j=0}^{12} y_j = 91 \qquad \sum_{j=0}^{12} z_j = 182 = 2 \times 91$$

$$[x_j = x(v_j)] \qquad [y_j = y(v_j)]$$

rather than tones, were used as the determining functions for assembling melodic structures.

As shown in the second column of Table 15, the harmonic function x_j was given values which run arithmetically from 13 to 1 in descending order of consonance. This simple arithmetic ordering was defined as an *unperturbed* set of weighted probabilities for the harmonic function. If these values are used directly for interval selection, this brings about, *on the average,* the selection of repeats thirteen times as frequently as the tritone, of octaves twelve times as frequently as the tritone, and so on. It was believed that this simple arithmetic scale of relative weights for the harmonic function would be an adequate representation of a neutral or mean position in terms of the imposition of tonal order. It is upon these values that we had to operate in order to perturb the *mean* harmonic texture, and thus achieve a higher or lower average degree of tonality.

In the third column, a similar set of values is tabulated for the proximity function y_j. It is seen that these values run arithmetically from 13 down to 1, as do the values for x_j, but that the *order* of the values relative to the stochastic variable v_j has been changed, so that the highest unperturbed weight is assigned to the repeat and the next highest weights successively to the minor second, the major second, and so on.

In the last column, values are tabulated for a third function, z_j, which is simply the sum $x_j + y_j$. This combined function was used in certain experiments to show how a simple combination of the two individual functions might be carried out. It is interesting to note that the two functions combined in this way yielded a scale of weighted probabilities that is, perhaps, not too different from conventional melodic writing. A statistical count of melodic intervals in appropriate examples of music might be of interest compared to this column.

Lastly, at the bottom of Table 15, there are given values for the sum of the weights for each function. These values were required for computer calculations to determine the frequency with which each interval occurred on the average. Thus, if x_j only was used to generate music, the relative frequency with which major thirds turned up, for example, was

$$x_4 / \sum_{j=0}^{12} x_j = 9/91 \doteq 0.1$$

or approximately ten per cent of the time.

Generation of Integer Weights. The values given in Table 13 were entered into the computer to constitute a set of weighted probabilities stored in the memory. As shown in Table 16, in which the information given in

Table 16

Assignment of Integer Weights to a Stochastic Variable

Stochastic variable, v_j	Integer weight, w_j
0	w_0
1	w_1
2	w_2
.	.
.	.
.	.
j	w_1

$j = 12$ in the calculations of Experiment Four

Table 15 is generalized, we could then assign any desired weights, w_0, w_1, w_2, . . . , w_{12}, to the possible intervals from unison to tritone. Having done this, we could then determine the sum of these weights, i.e.,

$$\sum_{j=0}^{12} w_j = W \tag{15}$$

and generate a random integer R within the limits $0 \leqq R \leqq W - 1$, as described previously under random-integer generation. The value $-R$ was then obtained and the weights w_j were added successively to this quantity *in sequence* until the sum

$$-R + \sum_{j=0}^{R} w_j$$

became positive. At this point, we took the value of the stochastic variable associated with the last weight added as the desired one. By this scheme, it is evident that the probability for obtaining w_j is w_j/W.

Changing the Weights of Transition Probabilities. The texture of music being generated by means of transition probabilities can be varied by changing the magnitudes of these probabilities in relation to one another. Thus, the "reference," or unperturbed, probabilities shown in Table 15 were operated upon in several different ways in Experiment Four, in order to see how changes in these weights would be reflected in the musical output. In practice, given values such as those shown in Table 15, there were essentially only two direct operations which could be effected, namely, making the weights more equal or, conversely, more unequal. Taking the harmonic function x_j as an example, it was possible to *subtract* unity successively from the unperturbed probabilities to remove the less heavily weighted probabilities one by one, the operation upon each x_j being terminated whenever its value became zero. In this way, we could gradually restrict the successive steps in a melody to the consonant intervals and eventually to just the octave and repeat, at which point fixation upon one note in the scale and, hence, upon a certain tonality was achieved. This technique could, therefore, be used to generate a type of harmonic drive toward a tonal center, while the reverse process is used to move away from a highly organized tonal center toward a less well-defined tonal organization. Naturally, it would also be possible to subtract or add larger increments than unity for more sudden shifts in musical texture.

A shift toward random music, in which all intervals are equally probable, was also easily achieved. This was accomplished by *adding* unity successively to the unperturbed transition probabilities until each one achieved the maximum value, namely, thirteen, at which point the value was fixed. All values for the weights, therefore, tended toward equality. Again, it would be equally possible to reverse the process and make the weights successively less equally weighted.

Both these operations were actually carried out, and the results thus produced were utilized to form the first two sections of Experiment Four.

Moreover, some additional experiments of this type, not included in the *Illiac Suite,* were also completed. It was also possible to subtract integer values from equally weighted transition probabilities—those for random music each having a value of thirteen—*in reverse order,* thus reducing the value for the melodic repeat first and the tritone last. In this way, we were able to obtain a set of inverse transition probabilities for x_j which produced music in which tritones occurred thirteen times as frequently as melodic repeats. This process was continued until all the intervals except the tritone were eliminated. This last was a species of music as highly restrictive as that which consists only of repeated notes. Samples of this output were generated by means of the Illiac, but were not included in the *Illiac Suite* because the previous results illustrated sufficiently well the general techniques of altering the weights of transition probabilities. The various operations described for altering transition probabilities are shown in Table 17.

Table 17
Changing the Weights of Transition Probabilities,
Utilizing the Harmonic Function, x_j,
as an Example

	Addition → / Subtraction ←		Addition → / x_j subtraction ←		Inverse subtraction → / Inverse addition ←			
Repeat	1	2 3 4 ... 11 12	13	13 13 ... 13	13	12 ... 2	1	0 0 ... 0	0
Octave	0	1 2 3 ... 10 11	12	13 13 ... 13	13	13 ... 3	2	1 0 ... 0	0
Fifth	0	0 1 2 ... 9 10	11	12 13 ... 13	13	13 ... 4	3	2 1 ... 0	0
Fourth	0	0 0 1 ... 8 9	10	12 12 ... 13	13	13 ... 5	4	3 2 ... 0	0
Major third	0	0 0 0 ... 7 8	9	10 11 ... 13	13	13 ... 6	5	4 3 ... 0	0
Minor sixth	0	0 0 0 ... 6 7	8	9 10 ... 13	13	13 ... 7	6	5 4 ... 0	0
Minor third	0	0 0 0 ... 5 6	7	8 9 ... 13	13	13 ... 8	7	6 5 ... 0	0
Major sixth	0	0 0 0 ... 4 5	6	7 8 ... 13	13	13 ... 9	8	7 6 ... 0	0
Major second	0	0 0 0 ... 3 4	5	6 7 ... 13	13	13 ... 10	9	8 7 ... 0	0
Minor seventh	0	0 0 0 ... 2 3	4	5 6 ... 13	13	13 ... 11	10	9 8 ... 0	0
Minor second	0	0 0 0 ... 1 2	3	4 5 ... 13	13	13 ... 12	11	10 9 ... 0	0
Major seventh	0	0 0 0 ... 0 1	2	3 4 ... 13	13	13 ... 13	12	11 10 ... 1	0
Tritone	0	0 0 0 ... 0 0	1	2 3 ... 12	13	13 ... 13	13	12 11 ... 2	1
	Fixed tonality		Unperturbed distribution		Random music		Inverse unperturbed distribution	Tritone music

Obviously, the same types of operations can also be carried out on the proximity function y_j, or for that matter on any other arbitrary selection of transition probabilities.

Zeroth-order Markoff Chain Music. In a monodic pattern, if successive notes are isolated and considered as such, it is possible to write music in which the choice of N_n is entirely independent of its relationship to note N_{n-1}. As we have seen, the mathematician calls a structure of this general type a zeroth-order Markoff chain—in particular species of random flight in which each successive event is independent of its relationship to the immediately preceding event. This would be zeroth-order Markoff chain music with respect to notes. A primitive type of relationship between notes, however, will be defined if we write zeroth-order Markoff chain music with respect to successive melodic *intervals* rather than *notes,* i.e., if we make I_n independent of I_{n-1}. Since we have already indicated in Chapter 2 that we prefer to think of melodies in terms of successive intervals rather than notes, let us define this as zeroth-order melodic writing. In zeroth-order melodic writing, then, a priori transition probabilities, such as those given in Table 13, are defined to permit moves from one note to the next and to permit the generation of sequences of melodic intervals. As we have already noted, the values assigned these transition probabilities establish the character of the music, but except for the unique case already considered of assigning a transition probability of unity to the unison (i.e., the repeat melodically)—or its harmonic equivalent, the octave—and zero to all other intervals to give rise to patterns of repeated notes, such music is intrinsically atonal, since there is nothing in the nature of zeroth-order transition probabilities to establish specific tonal centers. In zeroth-order Markoff chain music, a melody starting on C, for example, can move anywhere conditioned only by transition probabilities, and if such a melody arrives, for example, on F sharp, there is no compulsion to return to C or to any other note. Moreover, even if we weight most heavily the probabilities for consonant leaps, like rising and falling fifths, all that happens is that the apparent harmonic movement becomes slower. Conversely, the more we weight the more dissonant intervals, the more rapidly we tend to experience oscillations between more distantly related tonal centers. Thus, tonality as such does not exist in such a texture except as the result of chance. Zeroth-order Markoff chain music is the simplest type of order placed upon random-note music, but it still contains within its species all types of music from tonal through atonal and finally to antitonal music, such as certain types of tone-row composition. All such more highly ordered systems therefore arise solely as the result of chance events and not as a result of design. We can also conclude that the consonance or dissonance of successive melodic intervals depends on the average upon how transition probabilities are weighted. Zeroth-order Markoff chain music can appear highly consonant or highly dissonant or any mixture in between. Thus, the simplest order is imposed upon random-note music by weighting certain zeroth-order transition probabilities more heavily than others. In terms of information theory, random-note music is characterized by maximum entropy content, while the weighting of transition probabilities in any direction, as in Table 17, for example, decreases entropy by increasing redundancy. However, it should also be noted that the degree of consonance or dissonance has nothing to do with tonality as such, since the essential characteristic of tonality, in view of our comments in Chapter 2, is the recall of events before note N_{n-1}.

It is interesting to observe that a great number of the various compositional rules of traditional counterpoint and harmony are concerned with zeroth-order Markoff chain effects. Many of the rules of first-species strict counterpoint used to generate the music in Experiments One and Two illustrate this very nicely, particularly the rules forbidding certain types of melodic intervals such as sevenths and tritones. More generally, many rules of conventional harmony are also of this type, for example, the rules given for the resolution of dissonant chords to certain choices among consonant chords or possibly other dissonant chords. It is important to note that in so far as they are usually given, these rules are stated without reference to musical context, this being considered a separate problem.

In Experiment Four, three samples of zeroth-order melodic writing were produced to illustrate this simple type of musical organization. The three unperturbed transition-probability functions shown in Table 15 were used directly for this purpose; thus, the probabilities w_{ij} for selecting interval I_i were simply set equal for all values of i to the values x_j of the harmonic function, y_j of the proximity function, and z_j of the combined functions, respectively, in three successive studies.

First-order Markoff Chain Music. The simplest way to improve upon the structural concept of zeroth-order Markoff chain music is to make the choices of new melodic intervals dependent on what has just immediately happened, that is, to make the choice of interval I_i dependent upon the choice of interval I_{i-1}. This is an example of a first-order Markoff process, and music written according to this principle may be termed *first-order Markoff chain music*. In conventional music, there are examples of first-order Markoff processes among composition rules, just as there are of zeroth-order rules. Among the rules of counterpoint, the skip-stepwise rule and the forbidding of certain types of parallel motion can be cited.

Given the functions in Table 15, the question arose as to how we might use these functions to produce some simple examples of first-order Markoff chain music. From among the many possibilities, the following first-order process was selected: A rule was employed which was a generalization of the skip-stepwise rule previously used. This rule required that the choice of the new interval I_i would be weighted most heavily against the particular interval previously selected, I_{i-1}, and most heavily in favor of the interval most different from interval I_{i-1}. Thus, for example, if the previous interval I_{i-1} had been a melodic repeat, the new set of probabilities for interval I_i would be weighted more heavily against the choice again of a repeat than if the previous interval had been a major third or some other intermediate interval.

Addition is the simplest process for carrying out this type of conditional first-order weighting, utilizing the basic functions in Table 15. It was possible simply to add the weight of the interval I_{i-1} to all the weights of the interval to be chosen, to obtain new weights for the actual choice process. In actual practice, the weights $w_{i-1} - 1$ rather than w_{i-1} were added to w_j. Examples of this process are shown in Table 18, utilizing the harmonic function, x_j. It is seen that the probability for a repeat following a repeat was much less than for a repeat following a tritone. Conversely, the probability of a tritone following a tritone was much less than a tritone following a repeat. In general, therefore, with this treatment of the harmonic function, dissonant melodic intervals tended on the average to follow consonant melodic intervals, and, conversely, consonant melodic intervals tended to follow dissonant ones. A similar treatment of the proximity function y_j would have the effect of causing small intervals to tend to follow large intervals and vice versa, thus providing a generalized sort of skip-stepwise rule.

As in the case of zeroth-order Markoff chain music, three samples of first-order Markoff chain music were generated, again illustrating (1) the effect of the harmonic function alone; (2) the proximity function alone; and (3) the combined function. This function w_{ij}, therefore, was set equal in the three cases to $x_i + x_{i-1} - 1$, $y_i + y_{i-1} - 1$, and $z_i + z_{i-1} - 1$, respectively, according to the calculation pattern illustrated in Table 18.

Higher-order Markoff Chain Music. A second-order Markoff process is produced whenever a new choice is made dependent upon the previous two events; a third-order process arises when the choice depends on the previous three events; and so on. It is possible, therefore, to produce by such simple reasoning complicated interactions between a new event and

Table 18

Examples of How First-order Weighted Transition Probabilities May Be Computed, Using the Harmonic Function, x_i, as an Example

Previous interval I_{i-1}	w_{i-1}	$w_{i-1} - 1$	Possible new intervals I_i	w_i	$w_{i-1} - 1 + w_i$	$W = \sum_{j=1}^{13}(w_{i-1} - 1 + w_j)$	Probability $\times 10^3 =$ $\dfrac{(w_{i-1} - 1 + w_i)}{W} \times 10^3$
Repeat	13	12	Repeat	13	25	247	101.2
			Octave	12	24		97.2
			Fifth	11	23		93.1
			Fourth	10	22		89.1
			Major third	9	21		85.0
			Minor sixth	8	20		81.0
			Minor third	7	19		76.9
			Major sixth	6	18		72.9
			Major second	5	17		68.8
			Minor seventh	4	16		64.8
			Minor second	3	15		60.7
			Major seventh	2	14		56.7
			Tritone	1	13		52.6
Octave	12	11	Repeat	13	24	234	102.6
			Octave	12	23		98.3
			.	.	.		.
			.	.	.		
			Major seventh	2	13		55.6
			Tritone	1	12		51.3
. . .			.	.	.		.
. . .			.	.	.		

Table 18 (*Continued*)

Minor sixth	8	7	Repeat	13	20	182	109.9
			Octave	12	19		104.4
			.	.	.		.
			.	.	.		.
			Major seventh	2	9		49.5
			Tritone	1	8		44.0
.	.	.		.	.		.
.	.	.		.	.		.
Tritone	1	0	Repeat	13	13	91	142.9
			Octave	12	12		131.9
			.	.	.		.
			.	.	.		.
			Major seventh	2	2		22.0
			Tritone	1	1		11.0

events that have preceded it. Second-order and higher-order relationships between notes can be found in composition rules. However, a simple cascading process of this type would not produce musical output bearing recognizable relationships to normal musical structures as the relationships between notes become more distant. Therefore, instead of continuing by generating second-order Markoff music, we utilized another more relevant concept, namely, that of defining structurally more important and less important notes. This working principle, adapted from the ideas of musical analysis described earlier, was utilized to produce Markoff chain music in which the notes occurring on strong beats, arbitrarily assuming $\frac{6}{8}$ time, were made to depend on one of the generating functions, while the notes occurring on weak beats were made to depend on another of the generating functions. Four examples of music utilizing this principle were produced by means of the harmonic and proximity functions given in Table 15. The organizing principle of this music is illustrated diagrammatically in Figure 16, where it is seen that two samples each of zeroth-order and first-order Markoff chain music were produced by these more complicated interactions.

In Cases (a) and (c), the harmonic function x_j was used to control the successive choices of strong-beat notes, while the proximity function was used for the weak-beat notes. In this elementary way, we built up simple structures analogous to those suggested by the analysis of conventional musical structures. Specifically, the harmonic function was used as a longer-range structural function to block in larger tonal relationships, while the proximity function was used to provide melodic filler inside these larger units. In the remaining two examples, Cases (b) and (d) in Figure 16, the roles of the two functions were simply reversed. The proximity function, y_j, was now made the more structurally significant in order to provide musical examples in which the neighbor-note, or proximity, relationship was predominant.

Markoff Chain Music and Tonality. In Chapter 2, we noted that tonality in musical composition depends in its simplest form upon a recall of the first tone of a given melodic line. It is seen, therefore, if we compare this concept to the Markoff chain music thus far described, that none of the musical examples can be called tonal by definition, since in none of them was there defined a dependence of note N_i upon note N_1 once i exceeded the order of the Markoff chain process being applied. However, it is possible to define an ith-order process in which the controlled intervals are

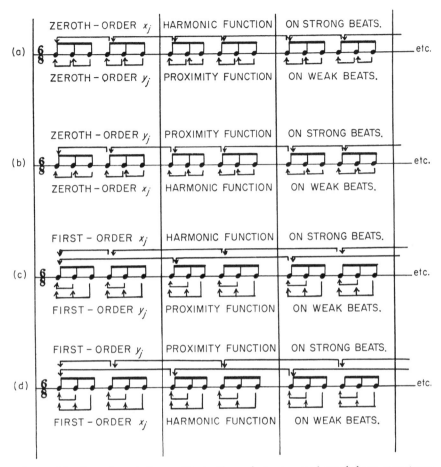

Figure 16. Experiment Four: Illustration of strong- and weak-beat structures utilized to generate species of Markoff chain music.

$N_i - N_1$ rather than $N_i - N_{i-1}$. Once we do this, we relate each new note to the initial note, rather than to the immediately preceding note. We immediately establish, as a consequence, the most elementary type of tonal control in accord with the simple definition of tonality just given. It is interesting also to note that zeroth-order and ith-order Markoff chain music bear a relationship toward one another analogous to that between the interval rows and tone rows discussed in connection with Experiment Three.

Therefore, in the last part of Experiment Four, a sample of ith-order music was produced, but in combination with first-order Markoff music. The harmonic function was used on the strong beats, assuming $\frac{6}{8}$ time, and was applied as an ith-order process. Therefore, each strong beat was related to the initial and, as we shall see, final note of this last sample of music. These notes were arbitrarily set as C in accord with the over-all tonality selected for the *Illiac Suite* assembled out of the musical examples. The weak beats were then assigned a secondary role, one of ornamental or melodic filler. This type of function was best expressed by the simpler type of Markoff process and by means of the proximity function, y_j. The musical pattern, therefore, was the one shown in Figure 17.

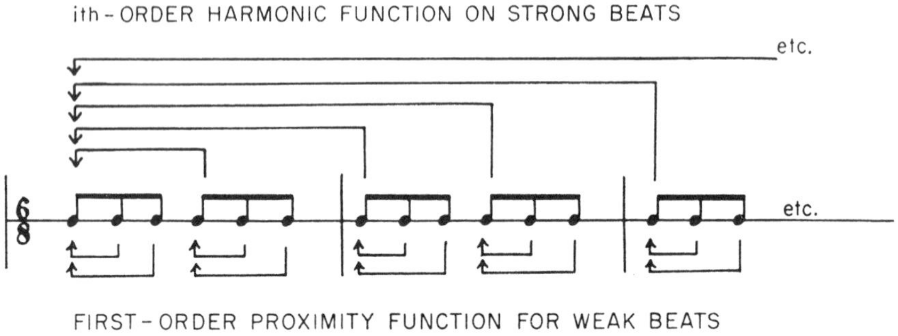

ith - ORDER HARMONIC FUNCTION ON STRONG BEATS

FIRST - ORDER PROXIMITY FUNCTION FOR WEAK BEATS

Figure 17. Experiment Four: Musical organization of the last example of Markoff chain music in Experiment Four.

Printout and Modulation.   All examples of Markoff chain music were arbitrarily printed in blocks of four lines at a time to permit transcription of the results for the four instruments, Violins I and II, Viola, and Cello. In this way, we were able to provide a maximum amount of musical examples in a minimum of score and playing time.

While writing the printing instructions for the Illiac for this last example, we also incorporated a simple demonstration of how modulation might be handled. Modulation can be defined as a shift of the reference point in an ith-order Markoff chain process to some new tonality. It is possible to design a simple program for resetting the reference point for the ith-order process after any desired number of measures, or, for that matter, after a randomly selected number of measures. Moreover, the new reference point can be preset, or it can be chosen at random, or by some sort of more elaborate, restricted choice process. For example, it might be decided that after

$m - 1$ measures, a modulation from C to F was required. Therefore, on measure m the reference point for the ith-order Markoff chain process would be shifted from C to F. To effect this, it would be possible to re-write the instructions for generating new notes. However, instead of re-writing the instructions, a simpler method involving the printout routine was employed, because it was evident that modulation is really nothing more than a transposition of the printed results. Thus, to shift from C to F, all we needed to do was to add the number 5 to each note while it was still in the machine as a number. This converted a C to an F upon printing, a C sharp to an F sharp, and so on, and yet did not disturb the basic note-generating process. It is seen that this is effectively what is done by any musician or composer in effecting a transposition or a modulation.

We selected the sequence I–IV–V–I, a simple cadence formula, to illus-trate this technique and combined it with the previously described tonal ith-order Markoff chain music to illustrate how modulation, as well as sim-ple tonality, might be achieved. Since C was selected as the fundamental tonality, the subsidiary tonalities became F and G, and the over-all tonal pattern produced became C–F–G–C. The shift to F was set to occur after six measures, the shift to G after another six measures, and the return to C after still another six measures. The use of a preset pattern of this type was preferred this time, since the use of more random processes for instituting changes of this type was amply illustrated by the musical examples in Ex-perimental Three.

Tonal Drive. Modulation is less commonly effected in a piece of music by an abrupt transition from one key to another than by a carefully and logically planned sequence of progressions which give the listener a sense of having arrived at a satisfactory resting point after the modulation is completed. Thus, for example, modulation from the tonic to dominant is a common feature of the exposition section in conventional sonata form. In a simple example of sonata form, the main subject solidly grounded in the tonic key is first fully stated. It is then followed by a modulatory sequence —often consisting of little more than broken chords—which convey the tonal weight from the tonic to the dominant, often through use of chords such as the dominant seventh of the dominant to produce a new resting point upon which the second subject is grounded. This modulatory section, to be convincing, must convey the sense of having prepared for the arrival of the new tonal center.

In general, this type of planning ahead in building up a tonal structure, which applies the concept of "tonal drive," can occur in modulation, as in the example discussed, and also at other points in a musical structure, such as at the close of a movement on a chosen tonal center. The chords preceding the end, therefore, would be related to the anticipated tonality, and the process in its simplest form would be a reverse ith-order Markoff chain, the reference point being ahead, timewise, rather than behind.

Thus, it was possible also in the last example of Markoff chain music to institute a simple process of tonal drive to a final tonality of C, utilizing a simple modification of the technique previously developed for changing transition probabilities. All we had to do was to reverse the process previously utilized to produce the first example of Markoff chain music as illustrated in Table 15. This process was, therefore, incorporated also into the instructions for this last sample of music. Unity was subtracted from the transition probabilities after every six notes (two measures), so that after twenty-four measures the only choice left became the melodic repeat. However, this technique, of course, was applied to an ith-order process on the strong beats, and, therefore, the only possible point of resolution was on C. A zeroth-order process, by comparison, might end on any tonality. In addition, the same process was applied to the first-order proximity function on the weak beats, so that weak-beat melodic skips were forced to become smaller and smaller on the average as the end of the cadence was approached.

A Simple Closed Structure. The combination of these techniques formed a logical group of musical entities which illustrate how a simple closed musical structure might be generated by the Illiac. Aside from the simple *cantus firmus* setting of Experiments One and Two, and the interval and tone rows of Experiment Three, no closed structures had yet been written to this point. Moreover, the *cantus firmus* settings and interval and tone rows represented really only rudimentary materials, which in most instances would be used for the building up of larger structures.

Therefore, the application of the harmonic function as an ith-order Markoff chain process on the strong beats and the proximity function as a first-order Markoff chain process on the weak beats, along with the process of shifting the tonal reference point after every six measures and the shift of the transition probabilities after every two measures by unit subtraction until only a melodic repeat could occur, permitted the production of a simple closed structure of twenty-six measures, which represented an extended cadence leading to a final close. This closed structure was utilized as a *coda* for the last movement of the *Illiac Suite* to serve as a simple prototype for building up more complex structures, such as conventional musical forms.

In general, in closing our discussion of Experiment Four, it might be noted that the actual coding of Markoff chain music was extremely simple by comparison with the programming of strict counterpoint. It was a completely efficient process, since there was no attrition resulting from the production of unusable notes; therefore, no try-again subroutine was required. It is entirely possible, however, that the discarding of notes would have to be resorted to once more complex interactions, particularly those involving cross relationships between the voices, were devised. The speed of production of the present examples of Markoff chain music was limited only by the speed with which output tape could be punched by the Illiac.

CHAPTER SIX

Experimental Results:
The Illiac Suite

Introduction

As noted in Chapter 1, the most satisfactory way to present musical ideas is in the form of actual sound. Therefore, as soon as we had planned Experiment One, we also chose a musical medium through which the results might ultimately be presented. The work described in Chapter 5 was sufficiently extensive so that a four-movement suite could be assembled out of the experimental results to parallel exactly the four major experiments. This piece of music, which we entitled the *Illiac Suite* in reference to the computer used for the experiments, is therefore a chronological research record of our experiments.

In assembling this suite, it was desirable to organize the raw results into a playable, relatively coherent whole. Moreover, it was also desirable to minimize the amount of arranging of the materials, so that as much as possible of the musical content of the suite could be said to be computer produced. This we have done, but in addition to the basic choices concerning which experiments were to be carried out, certain additional decisions were required during the transcription of the computer output to a musical me-

152

dium. These will now be briefly reviewed so that if the score of the *Illiac Suite* in the Appendix is examined, it will be clear what elements in the score result strictly from the operation of the computer and what elements have been inserted or adjusted as a result of practical necessity. The main problems involved in transcribing the experimental results were the following:

1. The first decision was the choice of a musical medium through which the results could ultimately be heard. The use of electronic or other synthetic means was eliminated in our case, since equipment of this type was not available. A conventional instrumental medium was therefore the only other reasonable alternative, but transcription for a keyboard instrument such as the piano was also eliminated because this would introduce the special restriction of having to have the music fit under the hands at the keyboard. Therefore, since, even in Experiment One, the objective was to produce a four-voiced polyphonic texture, the choice of a string quartet medium appeared logical and convenient; the problems in transcription would be minimized. Secondly, a string quartet has a fairly homogeneous timbre, which was desirable from our viewpoint; and lastly, the practical problem of having the music performed appeared less formidable than with larger or more exotic instrumental combinations.

2. Since much more musical output was produced by means of the Illiac than could possibly be used, it became necessary in each of the experiments to employ some sort of unbiased screening procedure to select representative musical output. It was important that we select impartially and not on the basis of aesthetic evaluation, since what we required were average rather than superior results. Therefore, various selection processes were employed, such as arbitrarily using every tenth *cantus firmus* setting, or arbitrarily selecting material at the beginning or end of a sample of output, or choosing examples at random by means of a random-integer table.

3. The choice of an over-all structure of a four-movement suite was made. The four movements were entitled Experiments One, Two, Three, and Four, duplicating the plan of the experiments themselves. Moreover, the internal structures of the four movements were planned to correlate with the details of the four experiments. The only self-contained musical structure produced completely by the Illiac is the last section of Experiment Four. This was utilized as the Coda of this last movement of the suite.

4. The choice of tempi for the four movements and in the individual parts of the first and third movements was made independently of com-

puter programming, since no programming for tempi was carried out. It should be noted that this is a simple problem, even with the inclusion of provisions for *accelerandi* and *ritardandi*. However, it was decided to select reasonably contrasting tempi for the movements and to defer the study of this musical problem in favor of other, more important projects.

5. It was desirable to transpose Voice 1, assigned to the cello, two octaves downwards relative to the notation utilized for the printed computer output; this was done to place this voice in the most favorable playing range of the cello. For the viola, used for Voice 2, the music was transposed one octave downwards, again for the corresponding reason. Voices 4 and 3 were played untransposed by Violins I and II, with the principal exception being in the first section of Experiment One, where the part for Violin I was transposed one octave upwards. Since the initial procedure for Violin I tended to place the music inordinately high in the playing range of this instrument, this transposition was subsequently abandoned.

6. Some subsidiary random-integer tables were utilized to select dynamic levels in Experiments One and Two and to distribute the *cantus firmi* and two-voiced settings in Experiment One among the instruments. Some doublings in these parts of this movement were also included to provide some dynamic variety. Also, certain restrictions to only two voices playing at a time were made in Experiment Four during transcription. This was done to add some variety to the musical texture of Experiment Four.

7. The meter for each movement or section of a movement was selected during transcription. In terms of computer programming, this problem is a simple one like programming tempo, and was deferred in favor of other projects.

Outside of several other quite minor additions, the rest of the content of the suite can be considered directly the result of computer programming. The general structural outline of the *Illiac Suite* is shown in Figure 18. The structural details of each movement of the suite will now be considered.

Experiment One

This movement is divided into three sections—*presto, andante,* and *allegro*—which contain successively samples of computer output which illustrate how we progressed from the writing of simple *cantus firmi* to two-part and finally four-part settings. In order to show a number of examples of each type of computer output, series of settings of different

Experiment One

Monody; 5 samples each of *cantus firmi* 3 to 12 notes long.	Two-part *cantus firmus* settings.	Four-part *cantus firmus* settings.
Presto	*Andante*	*Allegro*

Experiment Two

Four-part counterpoint; from random white-note music to strict counterpoint with rules added successively. Two samples of each type setting.	*CODA* Extra samples of cadences.
Adagio, ma non troppo lento	

Experiment Three

Basic rhythm, dynamics, and instrumentation code.	Random chromatic music.	Modified rhythm, dynamics, and instrumentation code plus random chromatic music.	Controlled chromatic music.	Revised rhythm, dynamics, and instrumentation code plus random chromatic music.	*CODA* Interval row	Tone row	Modified tone row
A	B	A'	B'	A"			
Allegro vivace	*Adagio*	*Allegro vivace*	*Adagio*	*Allegro vivace*	*Adagio and Allegro vivace alternatingly.*		

Experiment Four

Alterations of harmonic-function transition probabilities.	Zeroth-order Markoff chain music.	First-order Markoff chain music.	Separation of strong and weak beats.	*CODA* ith-order Markoff chain music; modulation and simple closed structure.
Tanto presto che possible				

Figure 18. Structure of the *Illiac Suite*.

lengths were strung together to form larger musical structures. Since these first programs for the computer were designed to produce fifty samples each of *cantus firmi* or *cantus firmus* settings from three to twelve notes long, the structures of the three parts of this first movement were designed to exhibit a sampling of all the output of the various different lengths. In the *presto* part of Experiment One, five samples each of *cantus firmi* from three notes to twelve notes long were used successively to build up this section of the movement. To provide reasonably unbiased sampling, every tenth sample of computer output was chosen arbitrarily for inclusion in the suite. These are played individually by the four instruments until near the end, where some doublings are permitted. The distribution of the *cantus firmi* among the four instruments was decided by means of a four-choice random-integer table, also generated by means of the Illiac. The scoring was carried out by associating each instrument with one of the numbers employed to build up the table. Successive integers in random sequence were used one at a time to assign *cantus firmi* to the instruments. It is interesting to note that this seems an entirely adequate way of scoring this type of musical material. The selection of dynamic markings was carried out by a similar technique. This time, the random integers were associated with the markings *ff, f, p,* and *pp.* Finally, as previously explained, octave transpositions were employed to place the *cantus firmi* into effective playing ranges for the instruments. At the close of this section of Experiment One, a *pizzicato* chord was inserted to show the transpositions used during transcription.

The second section of this movement (*andante*) is a sampling of two-part *cantus firmus* settings. Here we put together successively individual samples of three- to twelve-note settings and then reversed the order to provide a change of structure and, hence, some musical contrast to the first part of the movement. The selection of parts and dynamics was carried out as in the first part of the movement, utilizing the same four-choice random-integer table, except that, for the choice of the instruments, the integers were used two at a time.

In the final section of the movement (*allegro*), a group of four-part *cantus firmus* settings of increasing length make up the structure, repeating the plan of the first part of the movement. Dynamic markings were chosen as before. The movement ends with an arbitrarily chosen sample of the settings, in which we allowed the voices to hold notes over many beats in violation of the rule against successive repeats. Also, a final *pizzicato* chord, duplicating the ending of the first part of Experiment One, was inserted for structural symmetry.

It is evident, upon examination of the score of Experiment One contained in the complete score in the Appendix, that in these settings the rules employed for Experiment One are not violated. However, it should be kept in mind that these various *cantus firmi* and *cantus firmus* settings exhibit faults one might naturally expect as a result of the absence of the remaining strict counterpoint rules. This is not to say that many are not without some musical interest within the limited technique given the computer, but only that the strict counterpoint problem was still incompletely solved. Obvious musical faults, in terms of strict counterpoint, include the outlining of chords such as triads, sequences of melodic skips, six-four chords, and a number of other imperfections. For reasons previously mentioned, it was decided to complete our study of the strict counterpoint problem by writing improved settings of the type included in Experiment Two.

The musical content of Experiment One, of course, has other obvious limitations. Aside from the extreme simplicity of the melodic and harmonic style, perhaps the most important limitation is the absence of harmonic change. The whole movement rests squarely on a C-major tonality, which yields a rather unusual static but not necessarily unpleasant effect. An alternate procedure, which could have been carried out even at this early point, would have been to score the *cantus firmus* settings in different keys chosen perhaps randomly or by some predetermined scheme. However, since this would have been an added musical element not directly related to the main objective of Experiment One, the use of such a device was not considered.

Experiment Two

In this movement, as previously explained, we wished not only to show that we can write essentially correct first-species strict counterpoint by means of a computer, but also how the imposition of counterpoint rules leads to a clarification of the texture of purely random white-note music. Therefore, in Experiment Two, the *adagio* of the *Illiac Suite,* we have assembled a sequence of *cantus firmus* settings, all arbitrarily fixed at a length of twelve notes. After starting with two samples of purely random music, as each section of the movement is reached, the number of rules governing the choice of the notes is increased in accord with the plan shown in Table 19. The movement ends with four extra representative

Table 19
Experiment Two
Sequence in Which Strict Counterpoint Rules Were
Successively Added to Random White-note Music

Section	*Added rules*
[A]	Random music; no rules
[B]	Skip-stepwise rule; no more than one repeated note
[C]	*Cantus firmus* starts on C with C chord for opening; cadence on C with leading tone in one of the four voices; resolution of tritone in VII$_6$, e.g., $\frac{F}{B}$ must resolve to $\frac{E}{C}$
[D]	Octave-range rule
[E]	Only consonant chords permitted except for $\frac{6}{4}$ chords; i.e., harmonic sub-routine added
[F]	Parallel unisons, octaves, fifths, and fourths still permitted; melodic sub-routine added
[G]	Parallel fourths; $\frac{6}{4}$ chords containing tenth still permitted
[H]	Best counterpoint

cadences written by means of our cadence program. Throughout, as in the first movement, dynamics were chosen by means of a four-choice random-integer table, and the over-all structure and octave transpositions were worked out during the course of transcription.

Two passages from Experiment Two might be given special consideration in examining this music, namely, the random white-note music used to open the movement and the highly organized music used at the end of the movement. A comparison of these settings illustrates how order can be imposed upon random music by the logical processes described in detail in Chapter 5. Experiment Two, therefore, is a simple musical illustration of how the introduction of redundancy into a structure with a relatively high entropy content brings about a clarification of texture. Since the settings also became progressively more difficult for the computer to work out, this experiment also shows how redundancy reduces the information which may be communicated and how increasing the redundancy can only be brought about by increasing the amount of material which must be rejected.

This movement happens also to be one elementary example of how a high-speed digital computer can be used to experiment with musical problems in a novel way, since the writing of a sequence of textures in the manner illustrated would be difficult to do by conventional means. The composer unaided by a computer is not normally conditioned to maintain an unbiased attitude toward his output, so while he could write the random white-note music with the aid of a random-number table easily enough, beyond this point it would be difficult for him to cope with the problem of obeying only certain rules and letting everything else occur at random.

Experiment Three

Each of the three long fast sections of this movement is built upon the rhythm, dynamics, and playing-instructions codes described in Chapter 5. The first part of the movement is an example of how the simple version of these codes operates. The only addition to the computer output here is the insertion of pitch levels for the four instruments. These were selected by means of an arbitrarily chosen tone row, in anticipation of the Coda of Experiment Three in which computer-generated tone rows are presented. All other elements in the opening measures of Experiment Three are seen to be based upon computer output of the type shown in Figure 9. The output for this section was transcribed directly as produced by the computer, since no selection process was necessary in this experiment.

The first *adagio,* section [C] in the score, for which both the $\frac{3}{2}$ meter and *ff* dynamic level were selected during transcription in addition to the slow tempo, is an example of random chromatic writing. This is music of the highest possible entropy content in terms of note selection based upon the normal chromatic scale. It has a higher entropy content than the white-note random music of Experiment Two, since there are five more available choices per octave, namely, the black notes. This is truly atonal music of the most extreme sort, as we have noted already in Chapter 5.

In the second *allegro vivace* section of Experiment Three, this random chromatic writing is combined with the second, more complex rhythm, dynamics, and playing-instructions code to produce a rather highly complex dissonant musical texture. In combining these two codes together, it should be noted that only on the 1s, or "strikes," were the notes of the random music utilized. On the 0s, signifying "hold" or "rest," the notes were skipped. In this section, each random note produced by the computer was denoted rhythmically by an eighth note.

The second *adagio* section, section [G] in the score, illustrates what happens when the few simple rules of writing described in Chapter 5 are imposed upon random chromatic music. It is seen that this music is much more controlled than the music in the earlier *adagio* section. These results seemed to bear out our anticipation that the particular rules of writing selected would be efficient in imposing order upon the musical output.

In the third *allegro vivace,* this type of material is combined with the second rhythm, dynamics, and playing-instructions code. The same technique of combination was employed as used in the previous *allegro vivace.* This music, in some ways, resembles certain kinds of contemporary music. The continually dissonant but rather colorful musical texture, the use of complex rhythmic *ostinati,* the shifting degrees of rhythmic and dynamic independence of the four voices, the absence of conventional tonality as a structural device, and the nature of the melodic profile all suggest elements of twentieth-century style. Aside from crucial factors such as tonality, the major element missing is perhaps the use of imitation and melodic repetition as a structural device. Because of this, we started at one point writing a computer program for composing simple fugues in this general style but later set aside this project in favor of the studies in Experiment Four. It might also be noted that our choice of the tritone resolution as our one element of harmonic control happens to reflect Hindemith's definition of two basic types of chords—those without tritone and those with tritone.[1] The two chord types in Hindemith's system bear different structural implications. Our choice of this device happened to be arrived at independently and came in part from our experience with the counterpoint experiments. However, it is interesting to note in Hindemith's writing a similar emphasis on the importance of the tritone in structural harmony.

One additional point struck us immediately when we compared these results from Experiment Three with the output produced in Experiment Two. In these two experiments, we have contrasted two widely different styles—one bearing a relationship to sixteenth-century musical style, the other to twentieth-century style. One style is highly restrictive, highly consonant, but sounds quite simple, while the other style sounds dissonant and much more complex and difficult to decipher. It is important to note, however, that simplicity of style and hence accessibility bears an *inverse* rela-

[1] P. Hindemith, *The Craft of Musical Composition. I. Theory,* rev. ed., Associated Music Publishers, Inc., New York, 1945, pp. 94–108 in particular.

tionship to the freedom of choice. The simplest style requires the severest restrictions and has the highest degree of redundancy. On the other hand, simpler musical styles are by no means necessarily the easiest to write, since the difficulty of composition involved in making the best choices from among the many available in larger structures in a less restricted style is offset by the fact that more of the available choices are permissible in terms of the desired end effect. This is illustrated by the comparison of Experiments Two and Three. The work required to extract the type of order illustrated by first-species strict counterpoint was greater than that required to produce the last *allegro vivace* of Experiment Three; the programming was more complex and more difficult. For a structure of given dimensions, we may therefore suggest that, as a general rule, a more restricted style is more difficult to write, since fewer of the interactions between the notes can be left to chance; or conversely, more of the interactions must be precisely defined. This conclusion is compatible with a composer's experience in writing a highly restrictive sample of music, such as a counterpoint setting, in comparison with the writing of a more loosely organized piece of music in which the relationships are permitted to be much more casual.

The Coda of Experiment Three, section [K], consists of one example each of an interval row, of a tone row, and of the restricted type of tone row described in Chapter 5. Each row utilized was arbitrarily assigned as a solo to the cello and followed by the inversion, retrograde inversion, and retrograde forms of the row played on the remaining three instruments. As described in Chapter 5, these transformations of the row were easily produced in the computer by changes in the printing instructions in the computer code. The code written to produce these rows could, of course, be utilized in future experiments as a basic subroutine in programs to produce more complex serial compositions.

In reviewing the musical results of Experiment Three, we have felt that one point at which the results might have been easily improved is in the repetition pattern of the rhythm, dynamics, and playing-instructions code. Setting the index for this at a maximum of twelve measures made the music seem to us somewhat overly repetitive. Resetting this factor involves changing only one number in the set of instructions for the computer. This, of course, is a very simple matter. An index of about six measures rather than twelve would perhaps be more nearly the desirable value to select.

Experiment Four

In preparing the score of Experiment Four, the experimental results were transcribed directly as produced by the computer, since all samples of output were equally good. Fast tempo and $\frac{6}{8}$ meter were arbitrarily chosen to provide a contrast to the previous movements, and dynamics indications were inserted during transcription independently of computer programming. As pointed out previously, results were transcribed for all voices simultaneously to provide more experimental material in the score in playable form. These experiments in monody were transcribed, therefore, as pseudopolyphony. Indeed, it might even be noted that a compositional technique of this type has historical precedents of various sorts; for example, in the part writing in late medieval music.[2]

The first two sections of this movement illustrate how changes in the transition probabilities derived from the harmonic function change the character of the music. In the first sample of zeroth-order Markoff chain music at the opening of the movement, the transition probabilities are adjusted after every two measures, so that by the time this initial section is completed, a sample of every distribution from only the repeat being permitted to the so-called average distribution has been illustrated. This is in accord with the shifts in transition probabilities shown at the far left-hand side of Table 15 in Chapter 5. The net effect of these shifts is to cause the music to progress from a fixed C tonality to a rather free texture in which the statistical distribution of melodic intervals is in accord with the "average" or unperturbed distribution. In examining the transcription of these results, it should be noted that each two measures represent the first sample of a larger amount of computer output representing each type of distribution. Therefore, across the bar lines of every other measure, the rules are not observed.

The second group of results, section [A] of the score, is a similar series

---

[2] Thus, "Franco [of Cologne] states that whoever wishes to write a conductus should first compose his own tenor . . . and then add the *discantus* (i.e., the duplum); if a third voice is wanted, care should be taken always to have it in concordance with either the tenor or the *discantus* . . . indicating that . . . the parts were written one at a time, rather than simultaneously." (G. Reese, *Music in the Middle Ages,* W. W. Norton & Company, Inc., New York, 1940, p. 308). This type of construction, as a matter of fact, might be of considerable interest because it could serve as a connecting link between the Markoff chain monody produced in the present Experiment Four and full-fledged polyphony.

of extracts from computer output in which a progression from random distribution, that is, equal occurrence, of melodic intervals to the unperturbed distribution is illustrated. In this example of zeroth-order Markoff chain music, we progress, therefore, from a more random to more restricted situation as opposed to the opening part of the music.

The next parts of Experiment Four contain zeroth-order Markoff chain music first based upon the harmonic function above (section [B] of the score), then upon the proximity function alone (section [C] of the score), and lastly upon the combined function (section [D] of the score). This is followed immediately by a similar sequence of samples of first-order Markoff chain music (sections [E], [F], and [G] of the score) which serve structurally in the movement as an answering section. In the presentation of these samples of computer output, as noted previously, the number of voices playing at one time was reduced arbitrarily from four to two, except for the playing of the combined functions. This was done simply to provide some additional internal dynamic variety to this last movement. It is observed that the character of each of these samples of music is in general accord with the rules which govern its production. The harmonic function music is characterized by a preponderance of skips and broken-chord patterns; octaves, fifths, and other consonant harmonic intervals occur much more frequently than stepwise motions. On the other hand, the proximity-function music contains a higher proportion of stepwise intervals, neighbor-note motions, and fragments of scales. In general, the over-all character of this music is more melodic in texture. Finally, when the additive combined function is utilized in a first-order process, the nearest approach to recognizable melodic writing possible through utilization of this general technique seems to have been reached. The first-order process tends to promote a type of skip-stepwise rule, as previously explained, so that wide skips tend somewhat more than in the zeroth-order process to be followed by repeats and stepwise motions and consonant leaps to be followed by dissonant leaps, and vice versa.

The next several short sections of the movement contain examples of music in which the weak- and strong-beat functions have been differentiated, firstly in a zeroth-order process and then in a first-order process. Even within the limited set of results kept in the score, the operation of the composing scheme outlined by means of Figure 16 in Chapter 5 can be distinguished. Taking the two contrasting zeroth-order samples of music from sections [H] and [I] of the score of Experiment Four, we see upon extraction of the strong-beat notes from these samples, as shown in Figure

19, that the sense of the harmonic function predominates in example (a), while the sense of the proximity function predominates in the example (b). Moreover, an inspection of the complete examples in sections [H] and [I] reveals that the weak-beat notes have been selected in general accord with the computer instructions.

Figure 19. Experiment Four: Extraction of the strong-beat notes from samples of zeroth-order Markoff chain music in sections [H] and [I] of the full score.

The Coda of Experiment Four appears to disclose in a satisfactory way all the features expected of it as described in Chapter 5. The modulations worked out as planned, and the harmonic and melodic simplification develops measure by measure as planned until the end of the movement is approached. Toward the end of the movement, on the strong beats, only the notes closely related harmonically were permitted to occur, while on the weak beats, only neighboring notes were permitted, until at the very end only the tone C was allowed. All of this worked out in accord with the computer programming and indicates that the design of more complex closed musical structures might be started by using this simple prototype as a point of departure.

CHAPTER SEVEN

Some Future Musical
Applications

Introduction

It is convenient to define two general areas of interest which might be
considered in applying computers to musical problems in the future. One
of these we may describe as the theorist's field of interest; the other, as
the composer's. The theorist analyzes music written by composers to
characterize musical forms and how they operate. On the other hand,
the composer is more of an empiricist who seeks out new musical forms
which seem to him to be satisfactory. In attempting to suggest how various
new musical projects might be started from where we have left off, we
shall arbitrarily group our suggestions into these two basic categories—
the first related in general to the analyst's problems, the second to the
composer's.

Applications to Music Analysis

The fundamental role of the music analyst is to verbalize specific musical
problems so that aspects of musical communication can in turn be defined.

165

In essence, the problem for the musical analyst is to find the reasons why a composer accepts or rejects musical materials, and to this end, principles of musical aesthetics such as those reviewed in Chapter 2 have been gradually established. We have indicated, however, that much of the writing on aesthetics is not yet particularly precise—Langer's "significant form" is a case in point. We have also indicated that the investigation of specific forms, rather than general concepts, is to be preferred for the time being in seeking more precise definitions of musical concepts. This proposition follows from the argument of significant overlap of levels of communication proposed by Weaver, which we referred to in Chapter 2. The description of musical forms perhaps ultimately can be expressed in terms of information theory or some future equivalent, although, at the present time, application of this theory to musical analysis is perhaps still too recent to evaluate critically in any detail.

If we now tabulate various applications within this general field of interest, the following suggestions come to mind as representative examples of the large number of possible projects which might be carried out:

1. Perhaps the most obvious application of computers to musical analysis is the extension of the type of studies already illustrated by the *Illiac Suite,* in which we have applied the Monte Carlo method to the problem of musical form. As a consequence of coding aspects of this problem as numerical information and generating experimental results by means of a computer, a computer is made to behave as a specialized, but unbiased composing apparatus existing in a completely isolated environment, subject only to the controls and information the music analyst might wish to supply. In this application, a computer is an ideal instrument by means of which analytical ideas can be tested, since the investigator starts with certain hypotheses from which he formulates operating principles; he supplies this information to the computer; the computer then generates music based upon these principles; and the investigator then analyzes the results to further his investigation. This, of course, is essentially nothing more than a standard example of experimental scientific method, but the unusual thing is that computers provide a practical experimental technique for carrying out such research in the musical field. It can reasonably be assumed that in the future the combination of these techniques with the more purely theoretical and speculative studies in the musical field, such as those by Moles, referred to in Chapter 2, would be profitable.

In our work, Experiment Four, in particular, suggests a technique of how a new type of analysis of musical forms can be brought about. This experiment, the theoretical basis of which is contained in information theory and more generally in statistical theory, could only be carried out in a reasonable time with the aid of devices such as the Illiac. As an initial working premise for future studies of this type, it is suggested—with appropriate restrictions—that most musical compositions reflect a balance between the extremes of *order* and *disorder,* and that stylistic differences depend to a considerable extent upon fluctuations relative to these two poles. As a second working premise, it is suggested that interest in musical structures is achieved normally when fluctuations around some stylistic mean between these two poles are also subject to processes of organization and arrangement timewise within the structure. The testing of these two general premises through the technique of generating Markoff chain music would be a logical extension of the work of this type thus far completed.

2. In addition to these more general studies, there are many specific tasks of musical analysis that could also be carried out with the aid of computers. The analysis of specific musical styles following perhaps some of the methods cited on pages 133 and 134 is one example. For example, estimates of the relative degrees of order and disorder of different samples of music or different sections of given musical structures could be attempted. This is suggested since entropy seems to be a more useful variable than less well-defined concepts such as "harmonic tension." Characteristic melodic profiles for different styles could also be examined and codified. Studies of this sort would be of particular interest in musicological research, such as finding the determining characteristics of particular styles of historical interest. It is also possible that the results of such analysis could be used in a practical way to identify, to sort, and to catalogue old music—often a tedious and laborious task. Thus, for example, it might be possible to determine whether samples of music merely represent variants of one basic piece or fundamentally different pieces. With adequate analytical criteria, at least a major part of such a problem could be coded for a computer to permit automatic cross comparisons of the samples and subsequent sorting into appropriate categories. As a specific example, at the present time we are considering a project for transcribing, sorting, and reproducing French lute music in a complete modern edition.[1]

---

[1] D. Lumsden, *Un catalogue international des sources de la musique pour luth* (*Les leçons d'une étude des sources anglaises*), CNRS colloque, "Le Luth et sa musique," Paris, Sept. 14, 1957; T. E. Binkley, letter to Jean Jacquot, President of CNRS, Paris, based upon comments upon Lumsden paper just referred to.

Since there is a vast quantity of this music, it has been estimated that up to ten years will be required to do the job by ordinary means. It has been suggested, however, that instruments such as the Illiac could be used to speed up the process. It should be pointed out in connection with this problem that a similar application of computers has already been made in the field of Biblical research and also in the preparation of a concordance for the new revised standard version of the Bible.[2] It has been pointed out that it took thirty years to prepare the concordance for the St. James version of the Bible, while for the newer Bible, the same task was carried out in nine months with the help of a computer.

It should be stressed in this connection that such a project would include the automatic conversion of old music into modern notation in score form, along with performance parts, if desired. Utilizing a computer, this older music could be worked up rather easily and after final editing could be made available in modern copy. The first step in carrying out this project is the design and construction of a suitable musical printout mechanism of the types discussed in Chapter 4. Secondly, the most efficient utilization of computers for such purposes would depend on the development of adequate scanning devices for computers which would recognize printed and even handwritten letters and numbers. At the present time, research is being carried on to produce such scanning devices. This was given recognition in a recent symposium devoted to document reading, pattern recognition, and character synthesis.[3] When these devices become generally available, it should be possible to adapt them to the scanning of musical notation. In the meanwhile, transcription of musical materials onto coded tape or punched cards is an adequate substitute technique.

Other possible practical applications in musicology might include the use of computers to realize *continuo* and figured bass in Baroque music and to complete the part writing in older music where the music has either been left incomplete or some of the parts are missing. In this last application, as a result of informed statistical style analysis, at least a highly probable realization of the missing parts could be produced.

3. Another practical application in this general area, namely, to peda-

[2] A. Carpenter, "Amazing New Uses for Robot Brains," *Sci. Digest,* 41(2):1, February, 1957.

[3] L. Cohn, R. A. Kirsch, L. C. Ray, and G. H. Urban, "Experimental Use of Electronic Computers in Processing Pictorial Information"; T. L. Dimond, "Devices for Reading Handwritten Characters"; A. I. Tersoff, "Automatic Registration of High-speed Character-sensing Equipment," all given at Session IX of the 1957 Eastern Joint Computer Conference, Washington, D.C., Dec. 9–13, 1957.

gogical uses, should be mentioned. Several such applications have been suggested to the authors. On pages 128 and 129 the use of restricted tone rows as *cantus firmi* for counterpoint studies was discussed. Extensions of this work, such as the generation and cataloguing of such tone rows into different groups with characteristic properties, has been proposed by Robert Kelly, the author of the counterpoint method for which these tone rows are intended.[4]

The systematic generation of musical materials for teaching manuals for instrumental performance would be a second application of this type. The preparation of manuals for the guitar and the lute has also been proposed.[5] In this application, the coding would be based on guitar and lute tablature rather than standard musical notation, since tablature is in itself already a codification of the technical limitations of these instruments.

4. A final application to music analysis, we should like to mention, is the analysis of musical sounds themselves. This type of information would be particularly useful in the production of synthetic music by means of computers in conjunction with other electronic equipment. A very considerable knowledge of musical sounds and their physical constitution is, of course, available today.[6] Moreover, a large amount of information on how to process these sounds by means of electrical and electronic equipment has been built up through the development of sound-reproduction systems, broadcasting, and other commercial developments, to say nothing of the more experimental techniques reviewed in Chapter 3.

Musical sounds are, of course, extremely varied, and the analysis of timbre, attack, and other factors which make up these sounds becomes quite complex and is by no means completely understood. It seems possible that a computer might be useful in improving the design of sound-producing equipment in one significant way in particular. The analysis of sound could be coded as digital information, using standard techniques such as Fourier analysis and the like, and stored for computer utilization in permanent form, perhaps, on magnetic tape or equivalent high-capacity storage. Instruments such as the RCA Synthesizer might be extremely use-

---

[4] R. Kelly, private communication.
[5] T. E. Binkley, private communication.
[6] Typical books on musical acoustics are numerous and include H. L. M. Helmholtz, *On the Sensations of Tone*, Dover Publications, New York, 1954; Alexander Wood, *The Physics of Music*, The Sherwood Press, Cleveland, Ohio, 1944; C. A. Culver, *Musical Acoustics*, 4th ed., McGraw-Hill Book Company, Inc., New York, 1956; L. S. Lloyd, *Music and Sound*, Oxford University Press, New York, 1937; H. F. Olson, *Musical Engineering*, McGraw-Hill Book Company, Inc., New York, 1952.

ful as primary sources for acquiring such stored information, or, alternatively, the analysis of actual sounds might be carried out in a computer by reversing the flow of information through a digital-to-analog type device of the kind we will discuss in the next section. Basic programs for extracting this information out of storage and building up complex sound structures could also be developed. These synthesized sound patterns could be printed out as digital results and used to process sound by means of instruments such as the Synthesizer. Or, more directly, this information could be reconverted directly to sound, using the digital-to-analog conversion units of the type discussed below.

Applications to Music Composition

1. There are many practical problems of composition which require examination in order that the rather limited catalogue of compositional techniques thus far treated might be extended. We may note, therefore, just a few of the more urgent of these problems to illustrate the nature of what could be done: (a) the writing of computer programs for handling many of the traditional and contemporary harmonic practices; (b) the writing of more complex counterpoint programs, including programs for more contemporary counterpoint; (c) the correlation of elements such as rhythms and dynamics to note selection; (d) the use of imitation as a structural device; (e) the use of thematic and melodic recall and development; (f) the coding of factors thus far neglected, such as tempo, meter, and choice of instruments; (g) the writing of standard closed forms, such as variation form, fugue, song form, sonata form, etc. This last is of obvious major importance. Not only specific forms, but the more general problem of form needs to be considered here. The application of ideas such as Schenker's concept of chord prolongation and of Meyer's concept of purposeful musical motion would undoubtedly be useful in these studies, to say nothing of the possible results of analytical studies such as those proposed in the previous section. In time, it is conceivable that the handling of many elements involved in the writing of standard musical textures might be carried out relatively simply and efficiently with a computer. This would depend, of course, on the ease and precision with which these musical elements could be programmed and the information stored in sufficiently compact form. The extent to which this may become possible is, of course, a matter for speculation at present, so we can only suggest that music-writing programs might be designed to produce music efficiently

by utilizing, among other things, standardized "library subroutines" for standard musical operations, much as today standard subroutines are utilized for ordinary mathematical operations. In this connection, it is worthwhile to note that the writing of the computer programs themselves may very well be made more efficient. Since the time consumed in computer programming normally requires much more time than the actual time of computation in a computer, there is intensive research today into the possibility of computers themselves generating detailed computer programs from more general sets of instructions.[7] Therefore, if these new techniques are developed, there is no reason to suppose that they could not be adapted to the coding of musical as well as mathematical problems.

2. The organization of more or less standard musical materials in relatively novel musical textures, including combinations not easy or even feasible by other means, might be carried out. Some possibilities which come readily to mind include: (a) the use of different rules or even of different styles between different voices in a polyphonic texture; (b) the inversion of rules, forbidding what is now permitted, permitting what is now forbidden; (c) the development of new rules of operation for handling musical materials, such as subjecting tone rows to complex permutations based upon the concept of these rows as arrays spaced across 12×12 unit plots of pitch versus time. A project of this type could perhaps very well be founded on some of the permutational composition techniques referred to in Chapter 3. In this context, the totally organized music, also referred to in Chapter 3, would appear to be a composing technique particularly suitable for computer processing.

3. There might be developed sets of new organizing principles for musical elements leading to basically new musical forms. In the *Illiac Suite,* we have already provided a number of specific examples of how this can be done. The production of random musical elements, either notes, or rhythms, or scoring, is one example. This represents the opposite condition of totally organized music and, as such, becomes a formal element to be integrated into musical structures. More generally, the control of a precise degree of randomness and of the fluctuation of musical texture between order and disorder would seem to be more easily controlled by computer processing than by other means. Obviously, this development of a composing style consciously based upon this picture of musical structure could be of significance in developing an aesthetic not only related

---

[7] For example, see D. D. McCracken, *Digital Computer Programming,* John Wiley & Sons, Inc., New York, 1957, chap. 18 in particular.

to concepts of information theory, on the one hand, but also, on the other hand, of more general significance than such relatively restricted concepts as traditional harmonic music, the tone-row technique, totally organized music, and so on. Moreover, since the codes used for the Illiac are based in part upon random-number processes, these codes permit the computer a conditional sort of "freedom of choice," this "freedom" being the equivalent of randomness. The extent of this freedom could be made to depend on how much the aesthetics of music might be expressed in the most general terms. If a large number of highly specific rules, such as the rules of strict counterpoint, are given the machine, the freedom of choice for the computer to select musical materials is quite limited. Not only is the over-all aesthetic quality highly predictable, but the specific details of the music are rarely surprising. This is equivalent to saying that the redundancy is large. However, if a computer is supplied with less restrictive rules, then neither the general aesthetic effect nor the specific musical results are necessarily so predictable. One possible consequence of this is that the composer might no longer be preoccupied with selecting specific notes of the scale, specific rhythms, and other such details, but rather with more generalized sets of symbols, which would be used in turn for the generation and arrangement of the musical details in accord with the musical "message." This could result in a very different attitude toward specific musical details, and they might cease to have the importance we now attach to them. In fact, these details could easily be varied over wide limits within the same essential "composition," just as we now permit, to a greater or lesser extent, variability in the interpretation of music by performing musicians and yet recognize that this does not destroy the uniqueness of a musical composition. It is only fair to note, however, that if such a development were to occur, it would be a radical departure from the attitude prevailing at the present time.

Among the few experiments of this type not involving computers that seem to have been carried out recently are compositions of students of John Cage, such as Morton Feldman, who has written a composition entitled *Intersection No. 3, for Strings, Woodwinds, and Solo Cello.* In this work, Feldman permits a high degree of improvisatory choice by the performers, since the "score" is set down upon graph paper rather than in conventional notation.[8] A somewhat similar, but less extreme experiment has also recently been carried out by Gunther Schuller in a string quartet

---

[8] H. Cowell, "Current Chronicle, New York," *The Musical Quarterly*, 38:123–136, 1952.

composed for the 1957 Contemporary Arts Festival at the University of Illinois.[9] Thus far, in our experiments, this particular aspect of musical composition has only been barely examined in direct terms. The most conscious application of the idea of controlling the degree of chance events occurring in a musical structure was set up in Experiment Two.

Of perhaps more immediate interest is the further extension of new musical organizing principles related to the general concepts of information theory, such as the Markoff chain music in Experiment Four. More experiments along the line of Experiment Four could be carried out, particularly to develop cross relationships between the voices. It might be possible to start, as previously suggested, with a musical form in which one voice is defined as a quasi-*cantus firmus* to which the other voices are related. Another possibility might be to make direct use or modifications of the techniques suggested by Hindemith[10] by means of which he classifies all chords into six basic groups and each basic group into subgroups depending on the tonal strength of each particular type of chord. This provides a basis for setting up a stochastic variable for the tonal value of vertical note combinations. In turn, moreover, as successive chords are considered, this variable might be used to control the "harmonic tension" of the music as it develops in time and, more importantly, the incorporation of harmonic factors into musical structural units. Hindemith's system has the virtue of being simple and yet amenable to the type of musical propagation developed for Experiment Four, since it is particularly applied to what we have termed zeroth- and first-order chain processes. His ranking of the chords, which seems reasonable as a zeroth-order evaluation, could be valuable as an initial reference standard. Any other zeroth-order basis for grouping chords could, of course, be used just as well, depending on the type of experiments the coder had in mind.

4. Another project might be the systematic study of microtone music. In the past, because of the difficulties of understanding and building systematic harmonic relationships in microtone systems such as quarter-tone music and complex tunings employing microtone intervals to secure just intonation in all keys, and performance difficulties, this field has largely been neglected. Moreover, in the few examples of microtone music we have heard, the smaller intervallic movements seem to fulfill a coloristic rather than a functional purpose. The use of quarter-tones in Bartók's *Violin*

---

[9] W. S. Goldthwaite, "Current Chronicle, Urbana, Illinois," *The Musical Quarterly*, 43:390, 1957.
[10] Hindemith, *op. cit.*, pp. 106–108, 115–121.

Concerto and in Julian Carillo's *Preludio a Cristobol Colombo,* to cite two examples, seem to be cases in point. With suitable sound production means, however, a systematic study of the harmonic and contrapuntal relationships in microtone music could be carried out by means of computers. Similar studies could be carried out also on unusual scales and tuning systems, or even variable tuning systems in which tunings could be changed during the course of "performance." Variable tuning, of course, is the ideal technique for securing just intonation in all keys.

5. Perhaps the most significant application of computers would be the combination of computers with synthetic electronic and tape music of the various types reviewed in Chapter 3. This obviously is a natural and complimentary combination, since with computer music we are primarily concerned with organizing musical materials, while with synthetic music we are concerned more directly with the production of sound. Certain specific rather immediate results can be predicted. In future experimentation with computer music, the advantages of being able to produce the results directly in sound as well as in score form are obvious. Not only would the results be analyzed more efficiently, but the means would be available for producing quickly and efficiently the final desired musical end result. Moreover, in view of certain of the other projects outlined above, the experimentation would no longer have to be confined to musical materials for conventional scales, tunings, and instruments.

However, it is not only to the advantage of future experimentation with computer music that the combination of techniques should prove advantageous. There are specific limitations to the present means of production of electronic music of the types reviewed in Chapter 3, one of which is the time and labor required to prepare the music. This is a tedious business requiring painstaking effort. There is also at the present time the need for expensive and elaborate electronic equipment, such as the RCA Electronic Music Synthesizer, if a wide variety of sounds are to be provided. In view of what we have already said in regard to such equipment, it is obvious that the development of simpler equipment operated via computer programming would serve the composer's needs as well as the music analyst's. This should be an interesting engineering problem in itself, since it involves taking from the digital computer a signal representing some sort of musical pulse and converting this signal to output recorded directly on magnetic tape for playback on tape machines. Obviously, playback and distribution of musical output not intended for live performance would be much simplified. The problem of converting digital-computer output into sound is a typical example of digital-to-analog conversion, a field of interest attracting considerable attention at the present time. Digital computers as they are now constructed are incapable of "doing anything"; they simply supply answers to problems. On the other hand, the second class of computers, called *analog computers,* simulate by analogy, usually electrical, actual processes which may be mechanical as well as purely mathematical. Electrical circuits have certain properties which can be used to simulate addition, subtraction, multiplication, and division, and even integration and differentiation of mathematical functions. It is in recognition of this property of electrical circuits that we can build analog computers which operate upon continuous functions rather than discrete integers as do digital computers. Details of the principles of operation of analog computers can be found in standard reference works.[11] Digital-to-analog conversion is required in the present instance, since the output desired is recorded sound. The study of this problem could be initiated in several ways. For example, computer output might possibly be used to activate signals from sine-wave generators, which in turn would be fed to the recording head of a magnetic tape recorder. A second procedure would be to adapt one of the digital-to-analog converters now on the market, such as the digital-to-voltage converter manufactured by Epsco, Inc., Boston, Massachusetts. The combination: *digital computer, digital-to-voltage converter, and magnetic tape recorder* seems potentially the most satisfactory composing instrument in terms of the technology of today. In such a device, sound synthesis would be carried out mathematically in the computer. Tentatively, this seems to be a technique superior to that of activating devices such as the RCA Music Synthesizer by means of coded taped input prepared by computer programming.

A related problem is the notation for various types of synthetic music. As mentioned in Chapter 3, a notation has been devised for the *elektronische musik* produced at Cologne, but it also seems apparent that a more general notation would be desirable. This notation might, for example, be based upon the analysis of sounds in terms of digital information. The processing of this information in a computer by the composer to produce a written score as well as recorded sound should be highly efficient compared with current methods of composition. Yet another related appli-

---

[11] For example, I. A. Greenwood, Jr., J. V. Holdam, Jr., D. Macrae, Jr., *Electronic Instruments,* vol. 17 of the MIT Radiation Laboratory Series, McGraw-Hill Book Company, Inc., New York, 1958; G. A. Korn and T. M. Korn, *Electronic Analog Computers,* 2d ed., McGraw-Hill Book Company, Inc., New York, 1956. Also periodicals such as *Instruments and Automation.*

cation of considerable interest in this combined area of computer and electronic music would be the realization of music too difficult or too complex for performance by live performers. Not an inconsiderable amount of modern music verges on being almost too difficult to perform. Charles Ives' *Fourth Symphony,* for example, is a case in point, to say nothing of a large body of more recent works. It would seem that the threshold level of our ability to perceive complex rhythms and tonal combinations exceeds present performance capacities.

6. It should be mentioned, although not directly as a consequence of the present computer experiments, that certain mechanical aids to the composer might be effected by means of a computer. In particular, one great help would be the copying of parts from scores to eliminate what is now very tedious and time-consuming work. This could be readily accomplished once the scanning devices referred to earlier come into use. Moreover, these scanning devices could be used to read composer's written scores and convert them into sound as well as into printed parts.

7. It is also necessary to take note of one less attractive possibility, but one which must also at least be mentioned, since it is so often suggested. This is the efficient production of banal commercial music. For example, it is not difficult to conceive of programs for writing music of this sort to generate songs for juke-box consumption and similar uses, probably at a highly efficient and rapid rate. All applications of this sort, however, are nonartistic and fall outside the area of problems of aesthetic interest. Belonging in a somewhat similar category is the frequently asked question of whether synthetic Beethoven, Bartók, or Bach might also be produced by computers. The answer to this would seem to depend on the degree to which the elements of the styles of these composers could be verbalized, i.e., coded in a form suitable for computer programming. Appropriate statistical analysis of Beethoven's music might conceivably lead to the production of synthetic average Beethoven, just as, in a sense, the application of strict counterpoint rules can yield a reasonable simulation of average sixteenth-century style, *quite independently of whether computers or normal composing techniques are employed.* The goal rather than the means appears objectionable here, however. The conscious imitation of other composers, by any means, novel or otherwise, is not a particularly stimulating artistic mission. Moreover, this type of study is, in the final analysis, a logical tautology, since it produces no information not present initially. The statistical aspect of the problem should not be permitted to obscure this point. Reduced to its extreme case, this process would revert

to coding exactly the content of a specific and particular piece of music, feeding this information into a computer, and obtaining back from the computer exactly the same piece of music. It is obvious that nothing is accomplished by such an operation.

8. The preparation of computer music for other forms of communication such as the stage, films, and broadcasting might be of particular interest in the use of computer music in the combinations with synthetic music discussed later on. As noted in Chapter 3, financial support in Europe for experiments in electronic music has been provided by government radio stations. This support is given because of the possible exploitation of this other species of experimental music in broadcasting and related forms of communication. There is no reason to suppose that effective means of producing musical and sound continuity for this type of end use might not be carried out efficiently by one or another of the various means we have suggested.

Summary of Results

If we consider the various results included in the *Illiac Suite,* it seems reasonable to conclude that the basic objectives initially outlined for this project have been achieved. It has been shown that computers provide a novel means for studying and exploiting certain techniques of musical composition which can be utilized to produce both conventional and unconventional musical structures. Secondly, by applying new concepts it has been possible to illustrate how various musical forms and processes of composition can be treated from a new viewpoint with the aid of computers. In concluding this discussion, it is desirable to summarize what seem to us the more significant results of these experiments.

1. The elements of musical communication have been separated into those subject to analysis, to coding, and to transcription, namely, specific elements of actual musical structures, and into those more intangible elements which, in general, appear to elude highly specific characterization. It is only the first group of musical elements which were considered subject to coding and to experimentation with computers at the present time.

2. The relationship of information theory to musical problems was discussed to point out how this theory is useful in setting up a technique for musical composition with a digital computer. The specific technique of restricted random number processes was selected as that most desirable for the simulation of composing procedures.

3. The process of musical composition was then defined in terms of the extracting of orderly structures out of random materials by a process of selection and rejection. Specifically, the process of musical composition was regarded as a process of introducing redundancy into a random musical situation.

4. A technique was then devised for studying the processes of musical composition by means of an automatic high-speed digital computer such as the Illiac, the computer located at the University of Illinois. The technique depends upon the Monte Carlo method for generating random numbers. The notes of the scale are numbered in sequence upwards, and then the computer is used to generate random numbers which can be interpreted as the notes of random music. The effectiveness of musical rules in bringing order into this musical texture can then be studied by operating upon these numbers with mathematical processes which express rules of musical composition.

5. It has been shown that historically well-known compositional techniques, problems of current interest to composers, and even more novel processes of composition can all be investigated by this approach. In particular, four Experiments were completed in which the following four sets of problems were successively examined: (a) The writing of simple diatonic melodies and the writing of simple two-part four-part diatonic polyphony. (b) The writing of four-part first-species counterpoint. This problem was studied to provide an example of how a well-known compositional technique can be adapted to computer processing. (c) A study of the programming of rhythm, dynamics, playing instructions, random and simple chromatic music, and of interval and tone rows was carried out. This was done to demonstrate how a computer might be applied to modern compositional problems. (d) A more abstract formulation for musical composition, that is, the application of certain techniques of probability theory and, more particularly, of information theory to produce a number of examples of Markoff chain music, was examined. This last project was carried out to initiate a study of whether a more fundamental basis than the conventional rules of composition might exist for imparting order to musical structures.

6. Enough musical output was produced by the computer to permit the assembly of a presentation of the experimental results in the form of a four-movement composition for string quartet, which we have entitled the *Illiac Suite for String Quartet.*

7. Lastly, some suggestions, mostly based upon the results contained in

the *Illiac Suite,* have been presented to indicate how the present work might be extended both in terms of immediate tasks and in terms of longer-range, more speculative projects. Specific examples of applications in the fields of music analysis and music composition were proposed.

In retrospect, it is interesting to compare the techniques applied to produce music by means of the Illiac with some of the comments of Stravinsky in regard to musical composition quoted in Chapter 3. When Stravinsky spoke of art as "the contrary of chaos," and said that "we feel the necessity to bring order out of chaos," that "tonal elements become music only by virtue of their being organized," and that we must "proceed by elimination—to know how to *discard,*" he was speaking, of course, primarily in general terms rather than in terms of detailed specific method. However, it is pleasant to note how accurately these ideas do indeed seem to express the logic inherent in the process of musical composition and how, perhaps for the first time, some considerable measure of quantitative significance can be attached to aesthetic commentary. The net result in the long run can only lead toward a clarification of aesthetic criteria, the improvement of musical understanding, and the production of new types of musical compositions.

Appendix

On the pages following, the full score of the *Illiac Suite* is reproduced by kind permission of New Music Editions, 250 West 57th Street, New York. In reprinting this score, we have made two changes in Experiment Two (page 187). The first change is in the cello part at (F), measures 46 through 49 inclusive. A transcription error occurred here and the correct notes have been inserted. The second change is at (H), also on page 187. The parts have been rearranged to the original distribution as generated by the computer. The distribution originally included in the *Illiac Suite* had been used in an attempt to eliminate $\frac{6}{4}$ chords arising solely as a result of transposition for the various instruments, but since this is a mechanical effect leading to violations of this rule rather than intrinsic to the problem being solved, it really serves little purpose, and hence, upon reconsideration, we have eliminated this change.

ILLIAC SUITE FOR STRING QUARTET

I. EXPERIMENT NO. 1

(E)

II. EXPERIMENT NO.2

(A)

(B)

(C)

(D)

III. EXPERIMENT NO. 3

✱ WHOLE–TONE SHAKE

IV. EXPERIMENT NO. 4

TANTO PRESTO CHE POSSIBILE

CODA
(L)

DATE DUE

S